W9-BZN-807

BISON
BOOKS

THE PIONEER HERITAGE SERIES

SISTER
TO THE SIOUX

THE MEMOIRS OF
ELAINE GOODALE EASTMAN
1885–91

Edited by
KAY GRABER

UNIVERSITY OF NEBRASKA PRESS
LINCOLN AND LONDON

First Bison Book printing: 1985
Most recent printing indicated by the first digit below:
          6   7   8   9   10

Library of Congress Cataloging in Publication Data
Eastman, Elaine Goodale, 1863–1953.
  Sister to the Sioux.
  (The Pioneer heritage series ; v. 7)
  1. Eastman, Elaine Goodale, 1863–1953. 2. Santee Indians. 3. Da-
kota Indians. 4. Teachers—South Dakota—Biography. I. Graber,
Kay, 1938–
II. Title. III. Series.
E99.S22323 1978   970'.004'97   77-25018
ISBN 0-8032-6713-4

CONTENTS

ILLUSTRATIONS

following page 48

FOREWORD

In 1886, Elaine Goodale, a young woman of genteel New England upbringing and proven literary ability, went to Dakota Territory as a teacher in a tiny, isolated village on the Great Sioux Reservation. Her frontier was more than a geographical one, for she was a pioneer in a broad-based attempt to bring the Indians into the mainstream of American life. The military campaigns to subjugate the Indians now over, the task ahead was to fit them into the larger society. Government and church efforts were directed at teaching the Indians to live like their white neighbors—the obvious solution to the so-called Indian problem in an age of "melting pot" optimism and belief in the social as well as physical survival of the fittest.

Although Elaine Goodale shared the general convictions of her white contemporaries about the superiority of their culture, she had an ability, particularly remarkable in the late 1800s, to see her Indian friends sympathetically as complex human beings and to adopt aspects of their life style that she found admirable. During her five and a half years on the reservation she wrote copiously about the Indians and their concerns. "My songs of Indian life exhibit a pardonable coloring of romance," she later observed. "However, I [wrote] mainly in prose and with serious educational purpose—in other words, to turn out propaganda rather than literature."[1] Her numerous articles for eastern magazines and newspapers, if they were propaganda, were also reporting of the highest sort: literate, informed, vivid, and entertaining. The memoirs presented here, written in the late 1930s, were based heavily on those journalistic pieces. The Epilogue is taken from the author's introduction to *The Voice at Eve* (1930), a collection of her poems, which was reprinted as "All the Days of My Life" in the *South Dakota Historical Review* of July 1937.

Elaine Goodale's marriage in 1891 to Charles A. Eastman, a Sioux physician, ended her official career, but she never gave up her literary interests. She collaborated with her husband on nine books (most of which were published under his name) and was the author of seven of her own. In addition, she continued to write on current Indian matters and to review books about Indians virtually until her death in 1953.

A Note on the Editing

The editing of these memoirs has been confined to regularization of spelling, punctuation, and capitalization, and to supplying footnotes where additional information seemed desirable. In the version of the manuscript submitted for publication, the first three chapters of the original manuscript were condensed into one because they included a great deal of family history of interest primarily to family members. The chapter titles used here are the original ones.

---

1. Elaine Goodale Eastman, "All the Days of My Life," *South Dakota Historical Review* 2 (July 1937): 179.

Mrs. Ernst E. Mensel and Mrs. Sterling R. Whitbeck kindly provided a copy of the manuscript of their mother's memoirs and authorized its publication. The Elaine Goodale Eastman holdings of the Sophia Smith Collection (Women's History Archive) of Smith College, Northampton, Massachusetts, also include a copy of the manuscript, carrying the original title, "Little Sister to the Sioux." The photographs are all from Mrs. Eastman's private collection and are used here through the courtesy of Mrs. Mensel and Mrs. Whitbeck and the Sophia Smith Collection. John R. Giardino prepared the map opposite the opening page of the first chapter.

KAY GRABER

SISTER TO THE SIOUX

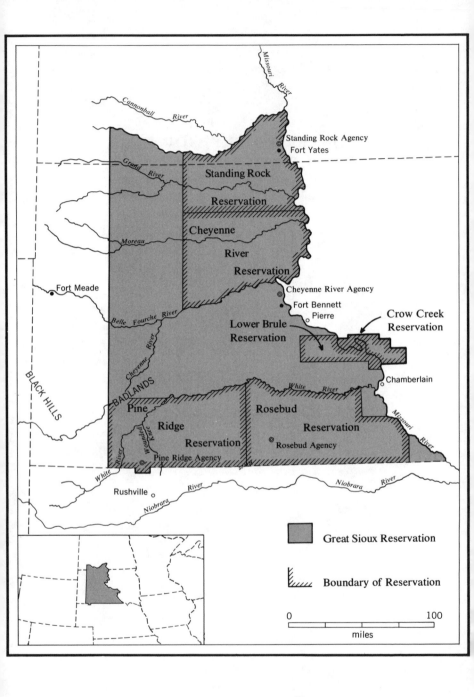

Standing Rock Agency
Fort Yates
Standing Rock
Reservation
Cheyenne
River
Reservation
Cheyenne River Agency
Fort Bennett
Pierre
Crow Creek
Reservation
Lower Brule
Reservation
Chamberlain
Pine
Ridge
Reservation
Rosebud
Reservation
Rosebud Agency
Pine Ridge Agency
Fort Meade
BLACK HILLS
BADLANDS
Rushville

Missouri River
Cannonball River
Grand River
Moreau
Belle Fourche River
Cheyenne River
White River
Wounded Knee
White River
Niobrara River
Niobrara
White River
Missouri River

Great Sioux Reservation

Boundary of Reservation

0   100
miles

PICTURES ON MEMORY'S WALL

MY FATHER, HENRY STERLING GOODALE, WAS
the seventh child and youngest son in a family of
eight, which traced its American heritage back to the
ancestor who landed at Salem, Massachusetts, in
1632. Yankee to the backbone, he was born in South
Egremont, Massachusetts, in 1836.

After graduation from the village academy he had
hoped to follow brother Sam to college, but he was
slight of build and the doctor advised against too
close attention to books, hinting at a threatened "con-
sumption." Instead, the youth was sent on a solitary
journey through the budding West and down the
Mississippi River by steamboat to New Orleans.

Soon after his return, on one of the long tramps
through the countryside he relished, Henry discovered his future home and true vocation. On a
rural road halfway up the mountain side in the
diminutive township of Mount Washington, he saw a
low-browed Dutch farmhouse facing a long slope of

[1]

sunny meadow, at whose foot curled a singing brook. Beyond rose ample pastures, and a triangular gap in the mountain wall disclosed an eye-filling vista extending the full sweep of the county; not another chimney smoke was in sight. Then and there the young man claimed that lovely and lonely prospect for his own.

It was not long before his father's generosity placed him in undisputed possession of the century-old farmhouse dwarfed by the inevitable great barns and with seven hundred acres of land. This was all equipped with cattle and tools according to the standards of the day. Each son must have his start in life, and this was Henry's. From that time on it was known as Sky Farm. Here Henry hopefully ranged himself among the pioneers in what was then rather contemptuously termed "book-farmin'."

In midsummer of 1862 Henry Sterling Goodale and Dora Hill Read were married. My mother was the pretty, youngest daughter of an old colonial family. Though straitened in means, they were people of some pretensions and she was a city-bred girl of fastidious tastes, unused to hard work and hardly born to fit so primitive a setting. She had a bright and active mind and a craving for the best things in life, both material and spiritual. All of her life she read, studied, and wrote—a born intellectual. With her trousseau of hoop-skirted silks she was brought home to a rustic brown cottage, solitary, in the middle of something like a square mile of half-tamed field and forest. Beauty was there—a beauty that meant much to them both.

The ancient farmhouse, solidly built, sat as close to the ground as a bird to her nest. There were four fireplaces, the great one in the kitchen unused since stoves were available. Most of the bed chambers were unheated, defying the fierce cold of a mountain winter. Water was all fetched in pails from an outdoor pump and wood from a shed close by. Kerosene lamps had to be trimmed, cleaned, and filled daily. Great washings were done by hand and hung to dry in the open air. Butter was churned by hand and bread baked at least three times a week. Such were a few of the routine tasks confronting a dainty city girl assisted, if at all, by a green Irish lass or the almost equally untrained local "help."

On October 9, 1863, in an upper chamber of Sky Farm, a daughter was born and was fancifully named for Tennyson's lovelorn Elaine. In 1866 my dear and inseparable companion, Dora, was born, and four years later my sister Rose. Our only brother did not arrive until I had passed my fourteenth birthday.

I have been told that I could read fluently by the age of three, a feat not so unusual then. Mother would not send us to the district school a mile or so away, and we had regular daily lessons at home. She was an accomplished woman for that era, with a taste for wide and varied reading which never failed, and I am glad to say implanted in us a genuine love of knowledge. An artist friend appeared at odd times to instruct us in botany and sketching, and one summer a visiting clergyman gave us lessons in Greek. Our education was overwhelmingly literary and humanistic. I was introduced to Shakespeare at the age of eleven and not long after to *The Marble Faun*, *The Mill on the Floss*, and *David Copperfield*—each a milestone! Long winter evenings are remembered in association with Gibbon and Macaulay.

Mother owned an old-fashioned square piano at which she often played and sang; however, poetry largely took the place of music in our later lives. She had a fluent and graceful pen, now and then breaking into print. My father's gift was equally distinctive. His bucolic masterpiece, a long dialect poem entitled "Does Farmin' Pay?," was many times recited in public before appearing in *Harper's Magazine* with illustrations by Frost.[1]

With this background and environment it was to be expected that rhyme and meter should come to us children almost as spontaneously as speech. I used to make up verses and croon them to myself some time before it occurred to me to commit them to odd scraps of paper. About the time that Dora joined me, she may have been around four years old and I, seven. We devised a magazine which we called "The Child's Monthly Gem," laboriously printed by hand and read to the family once a month. In the more mature form of "Sky Farm Life" it was continued into my eighteenth year.

Lacking schoolmates and companions of our own age and with few outside treats, ours was a tranquil and joyous existence, greatly preferable in some ways to the crowded lives of most modern youngsters. We learned very early to call upon our inner resources for entertainment and not only invented amusements for ourselves but planned original plays and other diversions with which to "surprise" our parents on special occasions.

It was an unwritten rule of the household that each member, however young, should if possible contribute something of general interest to talk at table. The idea was to make a good story out of a drive after the mail, a trip to the forty-acre lot to salt the sheep, a

---

1. The illustrator and cartoonist Arthur Burdett Frost (1851–1928) was known for his pen-and-ink drawings of rural American characters.

hunt for a hen turkey's nest, or a day's shopping trip to Great Barrington. Such events as my first visit to the theatre with my father—a ride "on the cars" all the way to New York, and an enchanted two hours of *Rip Van Winkle*—stand out brilliantly. Even the county fair with its crowds and fireworks and the thrill of winning prizes of silver spoons held a meaning all its own. Our little family circle formed a kind of private world to which only a few close friends were admitted.

I feel very sorry for a child who has not known real heart-warming intimacy with a grandparent or two. My maternal grandmother, Eleanor Lyon Read, lived in our home for the ten years before her death at seventy-six, which occurred when I was nearly fifteen years old. Left a widow in middle life with a large family of daughters and a small income, her strong happy nature had been refined and disciplined into rare sweetness.

Thaddeus Benedict Read, the husband of the once young and spirited Eleanor Lyon, has been described as a grave, bookish man with a strong vein of passionate melancholy. He was a direct descendant of the Hon. John Read, eminent lawyer and Queen's attorney, to whom the royal favor had been pleased to grant a certain manor of Lonetown, lying within the township of Redding (originally spelled Reading) in Connecticut. Mother was proud of the aristocratic tradition and her distinguished ancestor, and spoke of the father who died when she was very young with loving reverence.

Since my paternal grandparents lived in the Goodale homestead in Egremont, only five miles away, we saw them often. Grandma Goodale, born Sophia Bushnell, was injured in a curious accident when a train on the New York & New Haven was blown from the track by a strong wind. She died not long afterward in 1871, ever a faithful and devoted wife and mother, a kindly and loving grandmother.

My paternal grandfather, Chester Goodale, was a homespun citizen of sterling character. Having laid the foundation of a modest fortune in leather and hides, he in time owned valuable marble quarries and several thriving farms. One of these adjoined our home, and all through my childhood he used to drive his light buggy up the mountain about once a week to oversee his property and visit with us. Grandfather lived to the age of ninety-two in good health and, we believe, would have survived much longer but for a brutal attack when he was nearing ninety. A tramp set upon him in his own stable and inflicted severe injuries from which he never recovered. His was a strong, simple character of integrity—I was much attached to him.

We children never questioned the somewhat wistful motto which hung in the entry opposite our front door: "Hath Not Old Custom Made This Life More Sweet Than That of Painted Pomp." Still, even in the days when with a child's uncritical enthusiasm I held my home to be uniquely desirable, it was impossible not to gather that its primitive domestic arrangements had at first appalled an exacting and inexperienced bride. Yet love and pride and her wish to excel in every undertaking came near conquering even such mountain-high difficulties. I have watched her making soft soap, drying apples and sweet corn, trying out lard, preparing sausage and head cheese, and putting up quantities of delicious preserves. She knit stockings and sewed beautifully, making all our clothes in excellent taste. A deep cupboard built into the dining room wall was filled from floor to ceiling with her delicate French wedding china reserved for ceremonious occasions. No doubt they symbolized for her that elegance and distinction which she never ceased to crave in the midst of rustic simplicity, for there was in her nature none of the whimsical humor and gay adventurousness with which my father was endowed. As someone has well said, it is easier to be prosperous than to be civilized, and Henry Goodale was preeminently the last.

FIRST FLIGHT

IN OUR MODERN PROGRESSIVE SCHOOLS CHIL-
dren are encouraged, even taught, to write poetry,
with full recognition of the truth that such a gift is in
a measure native to the age of fancy and dream. Sixty
or seventy years ago there was solemn talk of the
"perils of precocity," and our parents were placed
more or less on the defensive as our accomplishments
gradually became known outside the immediate family circle. We, of course, wrote and recited primarily
to please ourselves, and they accepted the result with
much the same fond approval that children normally
receive, judiciously refraining from expressions of
surprise or extravagant praise.

As we grew older and improved in our work
through constant practice, my father began copying a
few of the best verses in his fine, individual backhand
and allowing them to be passed about in a limited
circle, quite without our knowledge. No corrections
were made, for both parents had sensitive literary

consciences, and at most would occasionally point out some flaw and allow us to mend it if we could.

These copies presently came into the hands of a gifted woman and writer, well known for her sympathy with child life—Mrs. Mary Mapes Dodge, who for many years conducted the magazine *St. Nicholas.* Mrs. Dodge wrote my father for permission to publish and received his rather reluctant assent. It was in the year 1877 that six short "Poems by Two Little American Girls" were introduced to the juvenile public in these kindly words by the veteran editor:

> Elaine and Dora Read Goodale, some of whose poems are here given to our readers, are children thirteen and ten years of age. Their home, where their infancy and childhood has been passed, is a large and isolated farm lying upon the broad slopes of the beautiful Berkshire Hills, and is quaintly called Sky Farm. Here, in a simple country life, divided between books and nature, they began almost as soon as they began to talk to express in verse what they saw and felt, rhyme and rhythm seeming to come by instinct.

Among Mrs. Dodge's selections was "Ashes of Roses," composed at the age of eleven, which has since been repeatedly set to music and sung in concerts by famous artists. I have rather resented the fact that these melodious but quite trivial lines have been chosen to represent me in various anthologies.

Our check from the magazine was for seventy-five dollars—in those days an unusually good price for poetry! Much more surprising were the letters that followed: letters from would-be correspondents of our own ages, from editors soliciting contributions, from autograph-hunters, and from interested and sympathetic readers.

A few writers of established reputation extended a cordial welcome, among them Emily Dickinson's first literary advisor, Col. Thomas Wentworth Higginson. "What miracles these young Goodales are!" wrote

Oliver Wendell Holmes to a friend, who passed on to my delighted father this word from the genial Autocrat of the Breakfast Table. It soon became inevitable that publication in book form be seriously considered, and there was no lack of offered advice, both for and against the step.

"We are wholly undecided," my father wrote to an intimate, "what course is best to take. I think at present we most favor keeping them from the public. I should never forgive myself if I did them an injustice in any way."

"We at first felt the natural fear," admitted the brilliant literary editor of the *Springfield Republican*, who became a family friend, "lest the stimulus hurt minds so young, but a better acquaintance with the influences that have formed and still surround them . . . convinced us that the common dangers do not exist in their case."

Apple-Blossoms: Verses of Two Children appeared under the Putnam imprint in the fall of 1879. It included about a hundred poems, none of which were composed before the age of nine years, and the engraved portraits of the young authors requested by the publishers. In her brief introduction, Mother spoke of the "almost unconscious outflow of two simple wholesome lives," offering to share them with "other kindly hearts that love true and simple things."

Our publishers, a conservative old firm, had not been sanguine of commercial success, and to us the warm reception of *Apple-Blossoms* seemed of a piece with fairy-tale fortunes and the gold at the rainbow's foot! The first edition actually sold out on publication, and successive printings brought the total up, as I remember, to nearly ten thousand copies. The contract, as it turned out, had been an advantageous one, and the sums added to the family exchequer by this and subsequent volumes must have been not unwelcome, since farming by this time had proved definitely a losing game.

However, I gave hardly any thought to this aspect of the matter, but was permitted to read the reviews that appeared in large numbers and were for the most part only too kind.

"So far as we know, without a parallel in literature," observed the dignified *Literary World*. "H. H.," then at the height of her fame, declared that "there has never before been a time in literature when a young thrush and a bobolink have printed a book!" There were friendly comments from the other side of the water. Said the English critic James Payn: "What strikes me as very remarkable about these poems is that they are not echoes."[1] The London *Athenaeum* described them as "delicate, sustained productions that need no apology on the score of youth."

> Hark! the breezes tremble
> With the sighs of April:—
> See her sweeping northward,
>   Spring! our Spring!
> Lingering, still we love her,
> Still we smile and beckon
> As we hear the rustling
>   Of her wing!
>
> Nearer, nearer, nearer!
> Dearer, dearer, dearer!
> Flying over onward
>   Comes the Spring.

---

1. Helen Hunt Jackson (1830–85), best known today for her exposé of fraud and corruption in the government's dealings with Indians, *A Century of Dishonor* (1881), and her novel *Ramona* (1884), wrote under the pseudonym H.H. Her *Verses by H.H.* was published in 1870.

A novelist and poet, James Payn (1830–98) was also editor of a number of literary journals, including the influential *Cornhill Magazine*.

What tho' cloud-veils sometime
Dim her eyes of azure?
Ah, the rarest pleasure
Tears may bring!

This is Elaine's spring song at twelve years. At about the same age sister Dora muses thus:

The azure sky is rich and deep,
    With fleecy clouds of snowy white;
The breezes sing you into sleep
    So gently on a Summer's night!

The whippoorwill, with plaintive cry,
    Rests from his eager, busy flight;
The dewdrops on the grasses lie
    And sparkle thro' the Summer's night.

The moonbeams catch the first fair flush
    Of budding June, with beauties bright;
The creamy, half-blown roses blush,
    Unfolding thro' the Summer's night.

Such lines were characterized by the staid *Atlantic Monthly* as "appealingly pretty little bursts of song." True, the America of sixty years ago was just a big, good-natured family compared with the sophisticated literary public of today. Its response was decidedly more sentimental than was evoked many years later by the clever city songster, Nathalia Crane, or the more naive and childlike Hilda Conkling.[2]

My father pasted letters and clippings into a set of scrapbooks, and I have no doubt took greater satisfaction in this wholly unexpected outcome of his romantic "Sky-Farming" than in any more personal success. Meantime, of course, we were growing up. Already the physical and emotional stresses of womanhood had begun to color every aspect of life. I had

2. Nathalia Crane was eleven when her collection of verse, *The Janitor's Boy* (1924), was published. Hilda Conkling's *Poems by a Little Girl* appeared in 1920, when the author was ten.

been deeply stirred by the birth of my brother (the inspiration of the "Baby and Mother" sonnets) and in that same year we lost our dearly loved grand-mother—my earliest acquaintance with death. About this time an unwise family friend embarrassed me profoundly by a premature declaration of love, even before I had put up my hair.

We continued to write for the magazines and put out three more little books, the last one half in prose. The critics found marks of advance and evidence that "these young poets have come to stay." We were carefully shielded from the curiosity of strangers. Metropolitan journalists, who persisted from time to time in making their way over the mountain in search of local color, were obliged to content themselves with meeting and interviewing my father. In this era of blatant publicity with motor tourists, radio, and motion pictures, I fancy such protection as we enjoyed would be impossible.

As it became clear that we needed more systematic discipline and a more disinterested atmosphere, at least one thoughtful friend had the courage to argue in favor of sending us away to a good school. However, I was already eighteen when arrangements were made for two terms in a small, select boarding school in New York City. Our schoolmates were hardly congenial, the teachers wholesomely critical, and we unaffectedly homesick. Nevertheless, by the end of the year I had made the necessary adaptations and should have been glad to go on to college. Mother had guided our later studies with the entrance requirements in mind, especially those of the new "Harvard Annex," as Radcliffe was then called. But the required funds were not forthcoming.

The truth is that I had grown up a nonconformist, indifferent to fashion and disliking the prescribed figure, firmly molded of steel and whalebone, upon which alone the costume of the period could successfully be created. An ardent votary of "dress reform" long before that movement had any general support, I insisted upon loose frocks and low-heeled shoes and rebelled against turning out my toes in the prescribed manner. It is tardy satisfaction to be vindicated, after many years, by modern ease and freedom in dress, and the correct position of the feet in walking!

Except for a determination to be comfortable, I cared little what I wore, seldom thought about my looks, and was socially abrupt and awkward—a fault which I have never been able entirely to overcome. I had no small talk, no particular desire to please, and resented the advances of an occasional "admirer" with disproportionate indignation. For these reasons, the few occasions on which our parents sought for us wider contacts were none too successful. I do remember with pleasure a call upon the poet Longfellow, whose kindly letter was among my father's treasures. I was seventeen when I went to my first and only college "prom." Never having learned to dance, I felt rather out of character in a frivolous pink frock, but was courteously piloted through the grand march by the class poet, who has since earned literary and academic distinction.

Both parents were about ready to give up the struggle. Mother, whose temperament was her greatest enemy, had become a nervous invalid, unable to attempt for the two younger children what she had in some degree achieved for us. Certain phrases were constantly on her lips: "the beauty of service," "plain living and high thinking," "our own duties and others' rights." In spite of their obvious failure to satisfy herself, I am sure that her idealistic maxims have influenced me deeply. It seems that I was educated in line with certain ultra-modern theories, which stress individual self-expression at a considerable risk of faulty adjustment to society.

SWING LOW, SWEET CHARIOT!

To RETURN TO A GLOWING MIDSUMMER DAY IN my fifteenth year—a gallant figure on horseback abruptly draws rein at the door of Sky Farm cottage and is received with unusual warmth by both parents. Our unannounced caller was General Samuel Chapman Armstrong, a man of great vigor and energy in his early forties, who had risen during the Civil War from the rank of a young lieutenant to the command of a Negro brigade. At the close of the war, he served under the short-lived Freedmen's Bureau, and this in turn led to the establishment of a vocational school for Negroes at Hampton Roads in Virginia, of which he became head.[1]

Armstrong's dramatic personality instantly gripped our imaginations. His shining countenance and rapid speech, overflowing with enthusiasm for humanity and bubbling with wit, proved irresistible. Even Mother succumbed. From the hour of that first auspicious

1. Armstrong had persuaded the American Missionary Association to establish the Hampton Normal and Agricultural Institute in 1868.

meeting under the lilacs, the famous champion of the
red and black races was no stranger in our home.

Only a few weeks earlier, in April 1878, Captain
Richard Henry Pratt's former prisoners of war,
tamed by kindness and eager to learn, had come to
form the nucleus of an Indian department at Hampton Institute.[2]

Either on that initial visit or a later one, the
General let fall an apparently casual suggestion destined to bear fruit some five years afterward. When I
was twenty the beloved farm changed hands. My
father took a salaried post in New York City and
Mother retired with the younger children to her
childhood home in rural Connecticut. It seemed up
to me, as the eldest, to try my unfledged wings.
Unwittingly, no doubt, she shaped my whole future
by her decision to accept for me the tentative offer of
a share in the Hampton experiment. The altruistic
motive appealed to us both, and a post in a missionary school was no doubt less wounding to her
pride than the alternative suggestion of tutoring
small children in a private family.

Hampton, at that time only fifteen years old, was
indeed based upon missionary notions of strict economy and personal self-denial. Salaries were nominal
and it was whispered that several of the staff had
volunteered to serve without compensation. In my
unworldliness, I remember envying those fortunate
souls, but circumstances compelled me to be finan-
cially independent. I was given my board and traveling expenses, and a very few dollars with which to

2. A military officer, Captain Richard Henry Pratt had been in charge of
seventy-two Kiowa, Comanche, Cheyenne, and Arapaho prisoners of war
interned at Fort Marion, Florida, from 1875 to 1878. He had begun an
educational program for the prisoners during their confinement, and
after their release seventeen entered Hampton Institute, where Pratt was
detailed to take charge of the newly created Indian department.

clothe myself with Quaker simplicity. I passed the summer vacations in Connecticut with the family.

An abiding faith in human nature, a selfless devotion to the cause of the needy of any caste or color—these were Hampton's foundation stones. Pure idealism was in the ascendant. Yet perhaps more than in any other school, either north or south, Armstrong developed the idea of labor as a creative and stabilizing force. This point of view helped to correct a marked predominance of the intellectual in my early training. True, we had all worked with our hands, on the farm or in the house, but Mother clung to the aristocratic tradition which tends to make this appear an unfortunate, if not a humiliating, necessity. At Hampton, I was first assigned to the sewing room and soon absorbed the prevailing gospel which exalted self-help and manual efficiency.

A pronounced individualist whose education up to that point had been one-sided, I was shy, reserved, and unsophisticated. The General and his helpers proved amazingly kind and understanding. Here, as Hampton's sweet chariot swung open to receive me, I first made friends of my own age, several of whom have remained friends for life. Here, as well as at Mother's new home, two or three nascent love affairs barely rippled the surface, leaving no profound effects. Absorbed in quite other ideas and plans, I was conscious of no unfulfilled emotional needs and thought hardly at all about marriage. I suppose I expected it to come, if ever, in the guise of pure romance!

The religious atmosphere of the school, which was undenominational, bordered on the puritanical, yet without asceticism. There were plenty of cheerful, innocuous amusements—country walks and talks, canoeing on the waterfront, a little tennis, an occasional oyster roast at Shellbanks or old-fashioned evening of music and games. Dancing was under the ban.

My first class was "adult primary," a dozen or so of earnest young men toiling painfully through first books in English. Some of them were older than I and desperately anxious to advance. Discipline was for the most part easy. Once, however, my tactless insistence that a six-foot brave stoop to pick up a dropped piece of chalk ended in a discomfited schoolma'am and the youth's casual exit by way of an open window!

The appearance of a slip of a girl in the role of taskmaster, issuing mysterious orders and requiring instant obedience, must have been to these potential warriors a bewildering anomaly. Much hung on our sympathy, ingenuity, and quick appreciation of the struggle to relearn, in maturity, such fundamental tools as a new language, new conventions, new social attitudes. It was a struggle of the will and the emotions, no less than of the intellect, in which both teacher and pupils engaged as pioneers.

Possibly, after all, my lack of any formal preparation for teaching was not wholly a disadvantage. I had early learned to think for myself and was handicapped by no stereotyped ideas or prescribed methods in the effort to devise a fresh and natural approach to the unique problem that confronted us in those days.

Hampton's Indian department, as may not be generally known, was a school within a school. Classrooms and dormitories were entirely separate for the two dark races. Except for the appealing Negro spirituals, sung for us in the chapel every Sunday evening, and the sight and sound of the trim, blue-clad battalion marching in to dinner to the stirring music of the school band, Indian teachers were in no way concerned with the hundreds of Negro students, both boys and girls.

The institution as a whole was dominated by the generous conception of human brotherhood implanted by its founder and head, a son of missionary parents in the Hawaiian Islands. The grave race problem posed by these aspiring sons and daughters of African slaves has stayed with me through the years, colored by the warmth and pathos of their artless plantation melodies—songs no modern singer can render with quite the simplicity of fifty years ago. Never, since then, has it been possible to think of the people of any race or nation as permanently inferior or essentially different. In this matter, the conclusions of science were long anticipated by the profound moral intuitions of humanitarians like Pratt and Armstrong.

The General's success as an administrator was due in no small degree to his keen appraisal of character, and his skill in setting others to work, seeking not so much to dominate as to draw out and harmonize our various gifts and powers. I had no more than begun to find myself as a teacher when I was encouraged to help publicize the novel experiment in which we were engaged. Public support was slow to develop and imperatively needed. It was our part to stage a popular demonstration of the red man's innate capacity. Our nearness to a fashionable winter resort led naturally to the irruption of floods of visitors, and these inevitably converged upon the more picturesque Indian classes. Some who came to scoff remained to pray, as the saying goes. Confirmed skeptics, on the other hand, must be effectively answered in cold print.

It was a short step from verse suffused with serious purpose to prose animated by the zeal of a recent convert. I was overjoyed to find the columns of *The Independent* and *The Christian Union*, leading journals of the day, hospitable to my budding enthusiasms. As an inexperienced girl of twenty, I did not hesitate a moment to enter the lists in public with reverend senators and other solemn graybeards, who in those days regularly inveighed against the shocking waste of public funds in a futile attempt to civilize "a horde of filthy savages." As well, they exclaimed, send coyotes and rattlesnakes to school as vicious Apaches and stolid Sioux!

I retorted with a story of heavily marked features that "lighten and quicken from day to day," of "rows of dusky faces fairly alive with every variety of expression," of "odd, bright questions and answers that make knowledge which before seemed hackneyed, even to one's self, a fresh mental acquisition." "Perhaps on no subject," I boldly asserted, "does the average Congressman display a more whole-souled, confiding and self-gratulatory ignorance than upon the Indian question!"

The General indicated his approval of my efforts by handing over to me the conduct of an Indian page in that excellent school organ, *The Southern Workman*. He saw to it that I had every opportunity to enlarge by reading and outlook. He even personally escorted a shy young woman, deeply impressed by the honor, to an early "Anniversary Day" at Captain Pratt's famous Indian School in the former army barracks at Carlisle, Pennsylvania.[3] With his usual magnanimity, he gave warm praise and encouragement to this

---

3. In 1879 Pratt left Hampton to open the Carlisle Indian Industrial School, which he headed until 1904. The most widely known off-reservation Indian boarding school, it continued in operation until 1918.

venture in many ways paralleling his own. Both men were Civil War veterans, both outstanding yet strongly contrasted personalities. Pratt lacked Armstrong's conciliatory manners and college background, but was his equal in energy, persistence, and single-minded devotion.

It was accepted doctrine with the leaders in this crusade of sixty years ago, including Herbert Welsh, Senator Dawes, and a few others, that a handful of primitives whose own way of life had been made impossible by our countrymen's advance could survive and prosper only through adaptation to the modern world.[4] They must walk steadily forward to economic and political independence. These men saw clearly that for them to remain small, subject groups, isolated in remote areas under the arbitrary rule of a bureaucracy, could only lead to weakness and ultimate degradation.

Education was the master-key and that education must be universal. A few favored strengthening mission schools with goverment funds, planting new local schools, and reinforcing every civilizing agency on the reservation. Pratt upheld the opposite policy and urged an adequate number of strong institutions in the heart of advanced communities. He would have these prepare their pupils, as was done at Carlisle, for entrance into the public schools and general life of the nation. General Armstrong advocated both plans and antagonized none.

---

4. A Philadelphian, Herbert Welsh was cofounder, in 1882, of the Indian Rights Association, one of the most influential of a number of organizations which promoted reform in Indian policy. These eastern-based groups believed that the Indians' only chance for survival in the face of the overwhelming encroachment of white Americans lay in their adoption of white civilization. They particularly emphasized the Indians' need to obtain formal education, espouse Christianity, dissolve tribal bonds, and become private property owners—self-sufficient farmers— through the allotment of reservations in severalty. Senator Henry L. Dawes of Massachusetts was the leading congressional spokesman for Indian reform.

THE CALL

BURNING WITH AN INTENSE DESIRE TO SEE THE
much discussed and little-known "Indian country"
with my own eyes, I took my problem to the General
in the middle of my second year at Hampton. With
characteristic generosity, he arranged at once for my
safe escort on a tour of the Sioux agencies in what
was the vast and thinly settled Dakota Territory. It
was the home of most of our early pupils, and I had
already begun to study their tongue from texts
prepared by pioneer missionaries. The last great
buffalo hunt was only a year or two in the past; the
Custer massacre, the sensation of less than a decade
earlier; Sitting Bull, starved into submission, had but
just abandoned his Canadian sanctuary to settle
down with sullen reluctance upon the Standing Rock
agency.[1] He was at that time by far the most famous
living Indian chieftain.

---

1. Sitting Bull and some three thousand of his followers had fled to
Canada following the Battle of the Little Big Horn. In 1881 he was
induced to surrender on the promise of a pardon and, in direct violation
of that promise, was confined at Fort Randall, Dakota Territory. After
two years' imprisonment he was released and settled on the Grand River
near the Standing Rock agency.

I was exceptionally fortunate in my traveling companions. My intellectual friend, Florence Bascom, who has since earned distinction as a geologist, had devoted a year to volunteer teaching at Hampton and was ready to share in the adventure. We met at her home in Madison, Wisconsin, where her father, Dr. John Bascom, was president of the State University, putting ourselves under protection of Mr. Herbert Welsh and a brother-in-law, officers of the then newly established Indian Rights Association. These "friends of the Indian" or "eastern sentimentalists," as they were called, hoped to reach some compromise with land-hungry westerners on the opening of the Great Sioux Reservation, and to this end conferred with leading Dakotans in Pierre, the capital.[2]

Our next stop, in that golden and memorable autumn of the year 1885, was timed to coincide with Bishop William Hobart Hare's annual convocation at Crow Creek. Here several hundred pious pilgrims from the "Seven Council Fires" held joyful reunion in a city of tents, after days of dusty overland travel.[3] While little English was spoken among them, their

2. The Great Sioux Reservation was established under the 1868 Treaty of Fort Laramie and was reduced in 1876 with the exclusion of the Black Hills. It comprised approximately nineteen million acres—about two-fifths of the present state of South Dakota—lying between the Missouri River on the east, Cedar Creek and the Cannonball River on the north, the Black Hills on the west, and the Nebraska border on the south. Six agencies—Standing Rock, Cheyenne River, Lower Brulé, Crow Creek, Rosebud, and Pine Ridge—served the reservation's Indians, who numbered about 18,500 in 1880. At the time of Elaine Goodale's visit, Congress had been under pressure for several years to open the reservation to white settlement; see note 6, below.

3. William Hobart Hare (1838–1909), was Episcopalian bishop of the diocese which included present South Dakota and the Santee Indian Reservation in northeastern Nebraska.

The term *Seven Council Fires* refers to the collective Sioux nation, which comprised seven subtribes organized into three major divisions—Santee (eastern), Yankton (middle), and Teton (western). The overwhelming majority of the Indians on the Great Sioux Reservation belonged to the Teton division.

friendly ways and dark, smiling faces made a pleasant impression. All were neatly clad in citizens' dress
and well drilled in the services of the church; indeed,
two or three had already taken Holy Orders.

Beyond the gently undulating high plains, in the
eighteen-eighties still for the most part unbroken,
their ripe grasses a-ripple under the strong sweep of
the prairie winds, lay a sluggish yellow giant—the
"Great Muddy" River. The sparsely wooded bottoms
were gay with goldenrod and the coral-fruited buf-
faloberry. The high, rolling bluffs, lovely to look
upon in certain lights when they took on melting
tones of violet and rose, stood out upon a nearer view
as barren sand dunes. There was no bridge at the raw
frontier town where the railway ended, and we
crossed the river in a rude ferryboat handled by a
yellow-haired Scandinavian oarsman.

From the Lower Brulé agency on the west bank, we
were driven over black, sticky "gumbo hills" to visit a
typical camp of "blanket Sioux" near the mouth of the
White River. A straggling collection of one-room log
huts dotted the grassy terraces above the junction of
the two noble streams, intermixed with conical white
tipis, brush arbors, and crooked stacks of wild hay.

At the heart of the forlorn little community there
stood dramatically side by side the symbols of two
opposed and irreconcilable cultures. The government schoolhouse, hastily put up some years earlier
in partial fulfilment of our solemn treaty pledge of "a
school for every thirty children," had never been
occupied. This dreary, paintless, broken-windowed
shack was neighbored by a smaller shack, the vacant
mission residence. Close by rose a stately new tent,
handsomely decorated and protected by a neat fence
of woven willows—the "Ghost Lodge," sacred to the
spirits of the honored dead.

The lodge contained a "spirit bundle" of hallowed objects, a raised dais for the repose of the departed, a cup and plate daily replenished for his refreshment. An old man, the guardian, remained in constant attendance.[4] But who would open the inhospitable doors of the waiting schoolhouse and ring the silent bell?

Joining his plea to the mute appeal of the ragged, neglected little folk who clustered shyly about us, came the kindly-faced chief, Medicine Bull. He had sent a son and daughter to Hampton, "so that they may some day come back and be my eyes." Here was a clear call to the heart of the ardent young girl—a call which she then and there silently promised herself to answer.

The next leg of our journey was accomplished by Missouri River steamboat. Those puffing, snorting little vessels which fifty years earlier had frightened the red men almost into hysterics soon after became indispensable both for passengers and freight, but at the time of our visit were fast losing business to the railroads. We boarded the *General Terry* at Pierre, where it took on bacon and flour for the upper agencies, and expected to reach Fort Bennett before dark. However, we soon grounded on a sandbank— an everyday experience—and passed most of the soft September night on deck, where the captain, in the intervals of "sparring off" and taking soundings, entertained us with hair-raising tales of frontier adventure.

4. The ghost lodge played a central role in the ritual of ghost keeping that was sometimes performed on the death of a loved one, particularly a favorite son. It required great sacrifice on the part of the family, culminating after two years or more in a giveaway, in which the family donated all its possessions to the needy.

After a night at one of Bishop Hare's model schools, surrounded by happy girls, we continued toward Standing Rock in a covered wagon with Indian driver, camping on the road, sometimes in tents, sometimes in a deserted schoolhouse or mission station. At Saint Stephens, we found the capable missionary at home and observed with satisfaction the progress made under his wise guidance. Most of the country was uninhabited, with stages or inns of any sort entirely wanting. Buffalo wallows and heaps of bleaching bones bore witness to the lately vanished herds.

Indians are expert in outdoor life, and their primitive arrangements delighted me. However, when we were later privileged to accompany the Bishop on his semiannual visitation to the Rosebud and Pine Ridge agencies, a two-hundred-mile journey in the episcopal buggy, with baggage wagon and extra saddle pony, some added refinements appeared. Sharing in the loving welcome everywhere accorded the church's honored head, we met and were hospitably entertained by his catechists and deacons at lonely prairie stations. Some were white men or of mixed descent. One or two of the latter had white wives, and one big, bearded German made us heartily at home with his large family of half-Sioux. We took part in all the special services and passed happy and profitable evenings about solitary campfires, made memorable by the Bishop's company and conversation.

Pine Ridge, our western terminus, affords a distant glimpse of the legendary Black Hills. Here we found several thousand Teton Sioux, the "wild men" of their nation, and a small group of their even more primitive allies, the Northern Cheyennes. The agent at that time was Dr. V. T. McGillycuddy (still living as this is written), a frontiersman of the old type, "quick on the draw" and a doctor of medicine as well.[5] To hear his talk was an education, for he was nothing if not a realist!

From Rushville, Nebraska, the nearest railroad point, we turned eastward, while my letters from the field, hurriedly written in longhand with no opportunity to polish, were already appearing in New York and Boston papers. Mailed at frequent intervals throughout the trip, they described in detail the semibarbaric spectacle of Indian camp and council, new to most readers, not forgetting to stress the effects of mission training with its promise for the future.

It was a critical moment in the history of the West. The pressure of a great immigrant population upon millions of as yet untilled acres—acres which government experts now tell us should never have been broken—had once more brought about an irresistible demand for the eviction of the Indians. Under the treaty of 1868 a huge area had been guaranteed to the Sioux "forever" and not an acre could legally be taken without the signature of three-fourths of their adult males. The notorious commission of 1882 had failed in an effort to buy the consent of a few chiefs

5. In 1881 approximately 235 Northern Cheyennes under Little Chief, who were unhappy at having been assigned to the Cheyenne and Arapaho agency in Indian Territory (present Oklahoma), were permitted to move to the Pine Ridge agency. Many of the Cheyennes had relatives there since the tribe had intermarried extensively with the Sioux, their recent military allies.

Valentine T. McGillycuddy (1849–1939), who served as agent at Pine Ridge from 1879 to 1886, earned a reputation for his uncompromising insistence on the Indians' compliance with the government's "civilization" program.

and mixed-bloods.[6] An executive order throwing open a coveted section in defiance of the treaty had been revoked. Now began a concerted pressure, through religious and philanthropic as well as political channels, to break Indian resistance and push the matter through. To the hard-headed frontiersman, the Sioux were hardly fellow-humans, merely obstacles in the way of progress. The more forward-looking champions of their human rights argued for land in severalty and citizenship, an end to the hampering reservation system.

Meantime, one young woman came home in spirit deeply committed to her task as she saw it. She had made up her mind to begin at the beginning, in the heart of a newly transplanted, leaderless, bewildered little community. Others could carry on in more solidly established institutions where there was ample support and companionship. Few, perhaps, would care to blaze a new trail in the obscure corner of a wild land, among recent "enemies" speaking an unintelligible dialect. Behind such considerations lurked, no doubt, a taste for adventure and a distinct bent toward pioneering, possibly handed down through a long line of early American forebears.

Before taking up duties at Hampton, General Armstrong persuaded me to tell my story at Lake

6. In 1882 Congress authorized a commission to negotiate with the Sioux for the relinquishment of some eleven million acres. When it was found that the commissioners had used tactics of intimidation and had concentrated on obtaining the consent of chiefs, ignoring the requirement of signatures of three-fourths of the men, new negotiations were ordered in 1883. The agreement obtained in the second round of negotiations was also rejected when an investigating committee headed by Senator Dawes found that the signers included a good number of ineligible youths and that many Indians had apparently not understood the proposal, and opposed it when it was explained.

Mohonk, where the famous series of Indian conferences had lately begun, upon the invitation of two
large-hearted Quakers, the Smiley brothers.[7] Again
at Newport, Rhode Island, I stood up in a crowded
church, without notes and almost without preparation, so full of my subject that the words fairly
tumbled on one another's heels. Here, a childless,
well-to-do Quaker couple actually offered to adopt
me as a daughter! But I was not to be so easily turned
from my purpose.

The broad-minded principal of Hampton listened
with what now seems to me amazing patience to the
hopes and schemes of a mere girl of twenty-two who
proposed to create a little center of "sweetness and
light"—so ran the intellectual jargon of the day—in a
squalid camp of savages. He made no effort to
discourage her or to utilize her passion for service
and propagandizing ability for the sole benefit of his
own needy enterprise. It may be that he perceived a
vein of Yankee common-sense behind the dreamy
gaze of the young crusader and poet.

"Go to Washington and tell the Commissioner of
Indian Affairs, Mr. [John D. C.] Atkins, just what you
have told me. Explain your ideas for an industrial
day school—a real community center among blanket
Indians. Here is a letter to the Commissioner," quoth
the General.

I penetrated to the presence without difficulty, but
did not feel that I got far with the whiskered poli-

7. The so-called Lake Mohonk Conferences of friends of the Indian,
inaugurated in 1883, were held annually by Albert K. and Alfred Smiley
at their resort hotel on Lake Mohonk, near New Paltz, New York. Albert
Smiley was a member of the Board of Indian Commissioners—a body
appointed by the President to review and advise on the administration of
Indian affairs—and the conferences, although they had no official standing, brought together leaders in the Indian reform movement in an
attempt to coordinate their goals and actions.

tician from Tennessee whom President Cleveland
had placed at the head of the Indian Office. I suspect
that he was more amused than impressed by his naive
and youthful caller. I distinctly recall his quizzical
smile and serio-comic insistence that I at least call my
"model day school," where I proposed teaching cooking, sewing, and gardening, as well as English and
arithmetic, an "industrial semi-boarding school."
Most people then believed that it was necessary to
separate the children entirely from their home sur-
roundings in order to accomplish results.

"You say you will serve a midday meal and you can
easily set up a couple of cots for emergency use,"
gravely explained Mr. Atkins.

One of the most gifted teachers on the Hampton
staff, my friend Laura Tileston, unexpectedly volunteered for the new enterprise. She was several years
older than I, more experienced socially, and her
unfailing flow of spirits under trying conditions
proved a valuable asset. But we could not induce the
Indian Office to appoint two young women to White
River camp. In this dilemma, Laura approached
Bishop Hare and secured from him a commission as
"lady missionary," with the understanding that she
was to share my chosen field on the wild west bank of
the muddy Missouri.

In view of the much stricter conventions of the
eighteen-eighties, it is not to be wondered at that our
families and older women friends strongly disapproved of the plan. "Young ladies" in that era rarely
ventured far from the beaten track, and a missionary
school in Virginia was quite unconventional enough!
Dire consequences were freely predicted in case we
persisted, ranging from attacks by the savages to the
cut direct from "Society" on our return to civilization.

WHITE RIVER CAMP

JUST ONE YEAR FROM MY FIRST INTRIGUING glimpse of a huddle of low brown huts mixed with yellowish cones, like sprouting mushrooms, on the banks of the dust-veiled Missouri, I found myself again on the ground, this time entered on the rolls as the first government teacher at White River camp.

Like most Indian agencies of that date, Lower Brulé was in appearance a rude prairie hamlet with only primitive conveniences, its row of cheap frame dwellings relieved from stark ugliness by a border of straggling cottonwoods and an impressive view of the river. Eight miles away, over the gumbo hills, agency carpenters were adding two small bedrooms to a 12′ x 16′ mission shanty, and making the whole more or less blizzard-proof with pine sheathing and building paper. A log annex in the rear must serve us for a kitchen until something better could be provided. A wing was tacked to the dilapidated school building for an "industrial room." While our future kingdom

was being made barely habitable in a leisurely, indifferent fashion decidedly trying to the nerves of a pair
of up-and-coming New England schoolma'ams, Laura and I enjoyed the hospitality of the resident
missionary (a full-blood Santee Sioux) and his wife, a
kindly German *hausfrau*. Their neat rectory, the
porch draped prettily with wild cucumber vines, was
colorful within, with choice examples of native art
and craftsmanship in striking contrast to the sober
plainness of the necessary furniture.

The Reverend Luke Walker, dean of the native
clergy, was one of the most interesting individuals I
have ever known. Tireless in energy, blunt in speech,
a fighter with a strong sense of humor, above all
unfailingly loyal and warm-hearted, he was in temperament anything but the conventional Indian. Together with Mrs. Walker, a very feminine person who
dearly loved to gossip and indulged in occasional fits
of "nerves," this devoted couple gave us the best
possible introduction to the strange new world of an
Indian reservation.

We found it, rather, two distinct worlds existing
side by side, now in dramatic opposition, now in-
timately mixed. There were already a few Dakotas at
home in the white man's world and superior in most
respects to the frontier white men. There were also a
good many of both races who belonged about as
much to one as to the other.

In ten years' residence at Lower Brulé, Mr. Walker
had built up a strong following of some five hundred
baptized persons in a population of about three times
that number. He was completely dedicated to the
work, prompt with instant response to a call for help,
by day or by night, and by no means limiting his good
offices to those of his own flock. Among other activities, he had organized a large club of men known as

the "Brotherhood," for mutual support in works of charity and friendship. Mrs. Walker, who had no children, led the women's groups and visited assiduously among the sick. It was no uncommon incident with her to be aroused from bed at daybreak with a request for light bread or fresh doughnuts to meet the craving of some exacting invalid.

The government Indian Service at this period was filled with Southern Democrats. They accepted the jobs in default of better ones, but had no great love for the red men, who in fact ran up against a distinct color prejudice. For this and other reasons we were more in sympathy with the mission element. However, common prudence would dictate an effort to keep on good terms with everyone, and my colleague's happy disposition and ready flow of amusing chatter went a long way in this direction. The agency people were never less than civil, though I must admit that their attitude sometimes suggested the kind of smiling tolerance one displays toward a pair of precocious—and occasionally troublesome— children.

Our first move toward better acquaintance with the sixty or seventy families in "our own" village was the long-range organization of a church sewing circle. Called together by the customary signal—a flag flown from the peak of the schoolhouse—the women hung back at first, unwilling to divulge their names. This racial taboo we easily circumvented by asking each one's name of her neighbor. Before long, the talk was flowing about as freely as in similar groups at home, with frequent bursts of happy childlike laughter.

Dear, lovable, intensely feminine Sioux women of days gone by! How affectionately I recall their devotion to their families, their innocent love of finery and gossip, eager curiosity, and patient endurance.

They wore straight, kimono-like gowns of brightly colored calico with wide, flowing sleeves. These were usually confined at the waist with a belt of leather and were short enough to display red or blue flannel leggings and gaily beaded moccasins. The inevitable shawl modestly draped head and shoulders. The younger women added a touch of vermilion paint on the cheeks and on the straight part between two glossy, forward-turning braids, with necklaces and bracelets of brass and shell. This rather oriental effect was on the whole more becoming than the fitted frock with tight sleeves adopted by the school-girls and some of the mission-trained. Moccasins were the last article of native dress to be discarded and the hat the very last "American" fashion to gain acceptance.

Soon the musical ripple and purr of the vernacular ceased to be strange in our ears, as we became able to join freely in the pleasant give-and-take of familiar intercourse. Prim-lipped mentors had gravely advised me not to learn the language, assuring me that I would often prefer not to understand what was being said. However, I found its acquisition a pleasure, as well as a real gain in promoting understanding and intimacy. Indian dialects are concise, pictorial, racy, and express certain ideas more accurately than we do in English—at least that is true of the one I know.

Only English was permitted in school hours (wisely, as I still believe), and hardly any officials took the trouble to learn Dakota. No one at that time, apparently, thought of helping the mass of adult Sioux to acquire ordinary conversational English, although this should not have been too difficult, and would have been of great practical use. The services of an interpreter, uneducated as a rule and often unreliable, were in constant demand, and I suspect this is still the case among the more backward tribes. We might well teach men and women "basic English" in a few easy lessons (say, among the Navajos) preparatory to its use in official dealings as well as in trade. Much as I once enjoyed speaking Dakota fluently, I am satisfied that the teachers of today do not need it. Utility, and not sentiment, should guide us in the choice of a medium of communication.

There were two roads from the agency to White River, the shorter and prettier winding through wooded bottoms, and in winter crossing wide stretches of Missouri ice, before turning almost upon itself to writhe up a steep, slippery hill to the top of the bluffs. Thence we overlooked the serpentine curves of the Missouri, the distant row of agency buildings painted white, and, still farther off, on the opposite bank, the straggling little town of Chamberlain. At the foot of a series of grassy terraces lay the Indian camp, bordered by a narrow black strip of fall plowing and a fringe of leafless cottonwoods. A tier of purple bluffs, with sharply defined shadows, formed an effective backdrop.

At least once a week we were driven out to meet with the women and observe the progress made by the carpenters—exasperatingly slow it seemed to us! On the first day of winter, December 21, 1886, we moved into White River Lodge with all our goods and chattels. Young [Sam] Medicine Bull, back from five years at Hampton, had been appointed church catechist and at once became our right hand. His duties ranged from reading the Dakota prayer book on Sunday mornings to papering our sitting room and improvising packing-box furniture on weekdays. Our black iron beds, straight chairs, and kitchen tables came from the government warehouse. A coal-burning heater was the more than welcome gift of kind friends in the East, who added a pretty blue rug, some dishes, and two comfortable chairs. Except for a housekeeper of years and discretion, imported from Chamberlain in response to the appeals of our respective mothers, there was no white person nearer than eight miles. A uniformed native policeman stood ready at our need to carry mail and parcels.

"One thing should certainly be mentioned to the credit of the 'heathen camp,' " I wrote to *The Independent*. "Axe, doormat, thermometer and other articles of value have been left outside from the first, together with some tempting lumber, and not a thing has been touched. No man, woman or child has intentionally annoyed us in any way, and for the rest—shall I confess it? Sam accidentally carried off the door-key in his pocket, and we slept that first night with doors unlocked, safe under the protection of the Stars and Stripes!"

True, only two or three persons in our village knew anything of house etiquette. We began by teaching them to knock before entering and to refrain from a preliminary peep in at the window. It was often necessary to clear the small room at dinner and bed time, for ours was the only clock in the place, and our many callers had no conception of regular hours for eating and sleeping. Since it was out of the question for us to follow the custom of serving food to all comers, at all hours of the day, we made a practice of inviting two or three neighbors to a meal at least once a week. This simple repast was to them a banquet, partaken of with dignity and propriety by men and women who might never before have sat down to a neatly spread table. When we, in our turn, went calling among the tipis, we accepted whatever refreshment was offered and strictly observed the native conventions.

We celebrated Christmas a week late, after several crowded days devoted to dressing dolls, filling candy bags, and marking gifts from the generous boxes sent us, in the intervals of setting our new home in order. A symmetrical cedar was brought into the school-room and adorned with the usual trimmings. Four in the afternoon of New Year's Day saw our snug abode full of friends from the agency, undaunted by a biting wind at 20 below zero. After coffee and cakes, the tree was lighted, the tattered flag set to fly above a broken bell, and a motley procession were soon taking their places on improvised benches under the direction of six former Hampton boys. We all sang the Dakota version of "Greenland's Icy Mountains" and all repeated the Lord's Prayer. Then what fun to strip the glittering branches while Sam read off the names, and little hands went up and brown faces sparkled, framed by jetty braids! Our first Christmas tree—the first these children or their parents had ever seen—can I ever forget it?

Next day, a troop of boys of all ages in ill-fitting suits of coarse brown duck—the despised government issue—their tousled black hair sticking out in all directions, roamed restlessly about, from time to time anxiously demanding when school would begin. The carpenters had left our school building littered with odds and ends of lumber and kegs of nails, a rusty old stove mounted on the platform for lack of enough pipe to set in position, about half as many seats as were needed, and one small, worn-out blackboard.

Spurred by the double tidings that the entire available force at the agency was cutting the year's supply of ice and that a Presbyterian lay teacher had just opened a Dakota school in a nearby cabin, we determined to begin at once without the promised necessities. A final appeal brought towels and soap and a small box of primers and crayons. I engaged an Indian couple to help, and that forlorn schoolroom was for once thoroughly cleaned! While Mark, mounted on a table, scrubbed walls and ceiling with an old broom, his wife scoured the desks and lower woodwork and I washed the windows. When the floor was reached the water barrel was empty. Mark got up his horses and hauled a second barrel of yellow river water. The lamps were lighted and Laura played lively tunes on the parlor organ—a recent gift to the mission—while I relayed hot coffee and doughnuts from the house. The work was finished by ten in the evening, when we two sat down to make a new flag and went to bed shortly after midnight, feeling ourselves equal to any emergency.

THE LAME HORSE BAND

IT WAS WELL THAT WE WERE NOT ENTIRELY DE-
pendent upon the indifferent or inefficient government bureau for needed supplies. Modern charts, a
new bell, later a pony and cart for extension work in
neighboring camps—these were some of the gifts
showered by eastern well-wishers upon our hopeful
enterprise. Boxes and barrels of good used clothing
shortly arrived, to be given to school children and
sold to others at a nominal price. The older girls were
supplied with dress materials and taught to make
their own. Nearly all the boys consented to have their
long hair cut on donning becoming new suits. Within
a few weeks we had our little folks neatly clad and
reasonably clean—at least during school hours.

We had gathered together almost fifty children
between the ages of six and sixteen, as provided by
treaty. Not one of them knew a word of English or
could read even in his own tongue—a feat made
comparatively easy by the limited vocabulary and the

strictly phonetic spelling of the Dakota language, as reduced to writing by the first missionaries. There were no family names, so for convenience we enrolled each child under the father's, adding the name of one of our eastern friends for personal use. These involuntary sponsors were later invited to take an active interest in their Sioux namesakes.

Schoolroom etiquette was formal in those days, but we varied it as much as we could with intervals of marching, singing, and simple calisthenics. When not otherwise occupied, the boys drew horses on their slates, while the girls designed patterns for bead-work. At noon, all were seated at two long tables in the annex, which had been furnished with a cook-stove (as well as a sewing machine), and were served in orderly fashion with a substantial meal. Milk and vegetables were unattainable, but we usually had a savory beef stew or rice with canned tomatoes, light bread or warm biscuit, and occasionally a tart made from dried apples or wild fruit. This noon lunch was a very popular feature, for although the Sioux were then in receipt of regular rations of beef, flour, and coffee, meals at home were sketchy and irregular. Besides, it gave the older girls practice in cooking, especially in making raised bread, a well-liked novelty.

When early spring came I put in a requisition for plowing, fencing, and seed for a school garden, in which the boys (the next year with the help of an Indian assistant) cultivated fourteen different vegetables, in quantity sufficient to supply three families—a valuable object lesson. Very few of our neighbors kept chickens and there was little or no game to be had. Since the government was beginning to issue cows which must not be killed for food, but kept for breeding purposes, I thought to make some use of my farm upbringing by teaching some of the men to milk.

"But the calf takes it all," was their first objection. "Do you want him to starve to death?"

"You must shut up the calf by himself," I instructed them, "and teach him to drink. Your own children need the milk." I knew families that stinted themselves severely in order to buy sweetened condensed milk for some unfortunate infant whose mother could not nurse him, often mixing it with weak tea or coffee, in far from sanitary bottles.

The men were not too polite to laugh heartily at the strange notion of a school for calves and it was up to me to demonstrate. This meant wrestling with an excited calf and a slopping bucket, as I had seen my father do, loftily ignoring a splashed frock and the delighted howls of a ring of masculine spectators.

Discipline was probably less of a problem than in the average public school, as nearly all our children were tractable and eager to improve. Most of the parents were cooperative. However, I recall one man who raised more corn than any other two in the village, yet would not send his attractive daughter to school.

"I put seed in the ground," he remarked, "and I see something come of it. You waste much time in play. I do not see anything grow."

However, one day the pretty little Scarlet Ball appeared in a soiled calico frock and attached herself to the school picnic about to set out in two farm wagons, armed with bells, whistles, and baskets of inviting food, for a flower-strewn meadow not far away. After that she took matters into her own hands, and turned up next morning ready to accept a new name and the trig summer uniform of blue and white checked gingham. Within two years our Florence read fluently in a Second Reader, sang sweetly, made good bread, her own dresses, and even her father's shirts.

"Now," admitted the one-time skeptic, "I can see that seed grow."

Community suppers, magic-lantern shows, and other wholesome diversions were a part of our plan, largely supplanting the native dances. Since these not only involve paint and Dakota dress, but revival of war games, late hours, and a general relaxation of all rules, church workers and conscientious government employees felt bound to discourage them. They were not, however, forbidden. Recent governmental policy promotes such amusements, notwithstanding they tend strongly to drunkenness, gambling, and sexual excesses.

Fifty years ago, a few strait-laced individuals needlessly rejected everything characteristically native without regard to intrinsic values. I was once taken to task by a good missionary of my acquaintance for habitually wearing moccasins in the house and about the camp. I am sure that same clergyman—if he had ever heard of it—would have rebuked me even more severely for taking part in an inter-camp game of "shinny" with a hundred or more yelling and excited men and women! Perhaps we placed undue emphasis on surface indications of conformity. On the other hand, there is no doubt that these help to bolster up the courage of the new convert and effectively advertise his change of heart.

"You remember all that has been said about day schools," Laura wrote to her mother. "Children would not come, clothes given them would be sold, and all such things. Well, my dears, just skip back a week and imagine us toiling up our hills in a big wagon—John (Hampton boy), Miss G. and I on one seat, as the back of the wagon was filled, first by a box of provisions, then, ice covered with straw, a bundle of tins for the cooking class—the paper bursting with the enthusiasm of the tins over their new mission in life, no doubt—two brooms standing up in high derision of conventionalities, and last but not least, a barrel!

"Miss G. had on a farmer's hat with no trimming, just purchased to keep off the blazing sun which we faced. Can you see us? Well, then, get home with us as fast as you can and open the barrel and find—fifty hats! So on Sunday, after church, I said to the children: 'Now all who want to throw away shawls and wear hats go into the house.' Down went the shawls and in they flocked like so many chickens, and on went the hats right and left, exactly the right hats turning up for the right chicks, until it seemed as if someone must have seen them all and fitted each. The old people stood about laughing and commenting happily. Then out marched our procession, shawls neatly folded over their arms and the pretty hats shading their eyes. I do not think I was ever happier."

Among the prophets of disaster, some held that no two women could keep house together and work in double harness without tears and temper. The omens proved mistaken. We divided the duties of school and mission, with each presiding over her own department and the other serving as assistant. "Miss Owl," as the Indians dubbed Laura, as sensible as she was merry, won instant popularity. There was no nonsense about "adopting into the tribe" with a story for the newspapers, but one day the old chief bestowed upon me in private, with a confidential air, the common and not too flattering nickname of his band—the "Lame Horses."

"How did they get that name?" I asked. "Well, it seems that once a long time ago, when we traveled far in a strange country, our people could go no farther. All our mounts were worn out or had sore feet. Since then we have been known as the Lame Horse band."

Should I have accepted the new handle as a compliment merely—or as a warning? I wonder!

All but two or three houses in White River camp were one-room huts with dirt floor and roof of sods, the last in summer blazing with sunflowers. Each cabin contained a cook-stove, upon which the coffee pot sat all day, two or more iron beds, and sometimes cupboards, chairs, and tables. The inmates habitually sat on the ground, and in summer cooked and ate out of doors. The hot, crowded little rooms were stifling in winter and insanitary at all times. I suggested an outside chimney with fireplace for ventilation, but the project did not materialize. A board floor and a shingled roof were usually the first improvements. I am sorry to say that recent reports from the Sioux country indicate that the average dwelling is little, if any, better than it was in my day, although the cost of schools has enormously increased.

There was a great deal of sickness, whole families succumbing to the plague of tuberculosis, against which no precautions were taken. Medical service was hardly more than a gesture in most cases, since the government physician was not supplied with transportation and rarely visited the homes. Hospitals and nurses there were none in the Indian field service. We early formed an alliance with our doctor, assuming responsibility for carrying out his instructions in

[45]

the case of children and babies, and I am sure we saved some lives in an epidemic of measles, then commonly fatal.

We not only administered medicines but prepared suitable food for our sick, carried it to their homes, and personally saw it consumed. We commanded them to stop in bed with fever, instead of dashing out of doors to cool off. Sometimes the present of a doll would keep a little girl quiet. Little babies perished in droves from exposure in winter, and in summer of dirt and improper feeding. As a last resort, there was always the native conjuror, with his noisy drumming and magic arts. If we banished the medicine man and the patient died, we, of course, were bitterly reproached. No attempt was made to penalize his well-paid activities.

Our housekeeper and chaperone was a good, motherly person, who tried hard to make us feel properly cared for. As soon as the weather made light frocks wearable, she used to say pleasantly: "I like to see my ladies in white." Just imagine dipping off the upper half of a hogshead of Missouri River water to "do up" the starched petticoats of the Victorian era! However, such things do help keep up one's standards in an alien world.

After all the children had recovered I came down with measles myself, and was rather seriously ill with that and an ulcerated ear. The only real hardships of those days must be laid to the combination of extreme cold and insufficient fuel. The first winter we burned green cottonwood in the schoolroom and I was often compelled to teach in my heavy coat, fur tippet, and arctics! In spite of everything I was happy.

A genuine thrill came with the annual break-up of the river. Once, at the end of a day's shopping in Chamberlain (including the *sinte*, or tail, a gift of candy or fruit after all purchases had been made and paid for), Laura and I were warned that the ice had softened so much as to be unsafe. But if we did not cross that night we should be marooned in town for days—possibly as long as a fortnight. What would our children do without us? With the rashness of inexperience we begged our driver to whip the team to a gallop and over the surface we sped, while long cracks rang out like pistol shots in our van! We made it safely—the last to cross that year. Next morning and for days after, clashing and grinding masses of heaped ice barred all passage until boats could again be used.

Then there was the famous blizzard of January 1888—not March as in the East. Two hundred Dakotans, most of them school children, were said to have lost their lives. Heroic teachers held their flocks all night, perhaps burning desks and benches to keep from freezing, while others tied the children together with ropes and set out for the nearest homestead. We dared not let any of ours out into the impenetrable wall of white, but fed and entertained them until toward nightfall the parents appeared, amused and grateful. It is believed that no Sioux perished that day, although many were abroad. No trains ran for weeks, which, for us, meant no mail from home.

Aside from our many Indian callers, who enjoyed the cozy room with the blue rug and gold-colored curtains and never tired of looking at the illustrated magazines we provided for their benefit, we had few but choice guests at White River. Once the woman superintendent of schools for Brulé County drove down on the ice. She reported "better fittings than in many of our white district schools" and commented on "an animated contrast to the stolid red man" in the person of my lively little partner.

Our first Episcopal visitation was a June event. We adorned the improvised altar with masses of creamy yucca and tall lavender foxgloves, marshaled our well-dressed, attentive youngsters into front seats, while proud parents and friends filled every nook and corner, and shared Mr. Walker's happiness in presenting the camp's first candidates for baptism and confirmation.

At this time Presbyterian and Congregational missionaries wisely united their ministrations among the Sioux, but there was some friction between this group and the Episcopalians, and even more between Catholics and Protestants, who thought nothing of deliberately proselyting one another's members. Wishing our people to think of other Christian sects as sister, not rival, organizations, we proposed a union prayer meeting on Sunday evenings, to be led in turn by lay teachers of the Presbyterian and Episcopal faiths and held in the schoolhouse, the center of our little community. The unconventional plan shocked some orthodox people and was promptly reported to Bishop Hare, who declined to interfere. Church jealousies and misunderstandings were common, and I am glad to remember that we did what we could to harmonize them.

It was a great privilege to entertain our Bishop, a lovable, broad-minded man. We had other honored guests—none more so than Hampton's great-hearted Armstrong, who wrote me after his return home: "I congratulate you on having found about the shortest road to heaven of all I know!"

Elaine Goodale, about 1880

Hampton Institute, 1886

White River mission, January 1887. Left to right: housekeeper; Laura Tileston, lady missionary; Elaine Goodale, teacher; and Dakota neighbors.

Elaine Goodale and day school students, 1887

Interior of White River day school

Chief Medicine Bull and his wife, Ina

Elaine Goodale with her driver and outfit, 1890

Day school on the Cheyenne River Reservation, with Elaine Goodale's tent and buggy in the left background

In the Bad Lands, 1890

Pine Ridge agency, 1890

Soldier stationed outside the Oglala
boarding school, Pine Ridge, 1890

Chapel of the Holy Cross, Pine Ridge, used as a hospital for the
Wounded Knee victims

Charles Eastman and Elaine Goodale, shortly before their marriage in 1891

CHANGING CUSTOMS

THE NAME DAKOTA, LOOSELY TRANSLATED AS *friends* or *kinsfolk*, covered seven or eight distinct bands of Sioux. They were not federated tribes like the Six Nations, but a people of one blood and one speech, with minor variations, and intermarried freely. When I first went to live among them, old customs were beginning to lose validity, but had by no means been forgotten. It was a period of changing manners and conflicting codes.

Extreme modesty, outwardly expressed in the averted gaze and hanging head, was the Sioux maiden's gauge of purity. An elderly chaperone, often the grandmother, was indispensable for all public occasions. No virtuous girl or young married woman might venture abroad unaccompanied. To meet men openly, look frankly in the eye, ride, walk, and talk with them and retain her reputation was, according to the old code, impossible. Yet, in our case, the fact was accepted without question. No smallest failure of respect in all the years in which I moved familiarly among them ever warned me of possible danger. The event proved that our trust in the native chivalry of the Dakotas was not misplaced.

Our women friends were more plain-spoken than the men, yet not offensively so. They invariably inquired our ages and openly marveled that we had been able to remain single so long. If we took up their babies to pet and play with, they sometimes laughingly suggested: "Why not have one of your own?" Their affairs of the heart were confided with a frankness that occasionally proved embarrassing.

A village coquette begged me to decide for her between two persistent suitors. Traditionally, a wedding was a family matter, to be arranged with some formality between the respective kin. Courtships were brief or omitted altogether. However, my own more romantic ideas led me to urge a decision on the basis of the girl's personal preference.

Having at last, I supposed, extorted a shy confession, I thought the matter settled and set to work on a wedding dress. Long engagements were unheard of, and in fact the young man's parents, prominent people in our little community, had already sent out a general invitation to the marriage feast.

Early next morning we were shocked to hear that the damsel had eloped overnight with her other admirer, to the noisy indignation of the family and friends of the flouted bridegroom. Nothing could be done about it, however, since the couple had taken care to have the knot securely tied at daybreak, arousing the minister from bed for the purpose.

Indian marriages, without other than a more or less public exchange of gifts, were recognized as legal for ordinary purposes, although both missionaries and government officials urged the conventional church wedding. Occasional plural marriages among the older men were condoned, but young people who had been to school and were, therefore, presumed to know better might be confined in the guardhouse for irregular conduct.

I recall one not-so-youthful widow who came to me in strict confidence as her "younger sister"—kinship names were generally resorted to among the warm-hearted Dakotas—entreating my help in arranging for a wedding ceremony. The intended groom was a widower a few years her junior. Her uncle, it seemed, had acted as go-between; she had never spoken with the man in her life and to do so now would be unthinkable. He was a pagan, but she had lately been baptized and wished to be married in church. Would I see him at once and gain his consent, since he fully expected to take her home that very evening?

I found the lover lounging in his tent, apparently overcome with shyness, disposed of the preliminaries in few words, and dispatched a messenger on horse-back to beg the instant attendance of our devoted pastor. Mr. Walker arrived within an incredibly short time, his shaggy little ponies all a-lather. We rang the bell and waited, not without anxiety, for the couple to appear.

They came and with them a goodly congregation. The bride shrouded her blushes in her heavy shawl, and not even the minister could hear her responses. We had hurriedly planned a modest wedding supper in our home, but to our discomfiture our friends were hardly pronounced man and wife when both escaped from the schoolhouse and made off rapidly in opposite directions.

A wedding in a Christian settlement, considerably more advanced than ours, illustrated the next step in a process of gradual adaptation to new standards. It was a brilliant midwinter day, with a savage wind, and the mercury far below zero. Mr. and Mrs. Walker called for us in their well-upholstered sleigh, where we buried ourselves in "comforts" and buffalo robes, our heads swathed in shawls and hot soap-stones at our feet. The twenty-mile drive behind gaily jingling bells up the ice-bound Missouri was further enlivened by stories of the ever dreaded air holes waiting under a smooth mound of snow to swallow up the unsuspecting traveler.

At the bride's home, a comfortable, double log house, we found that no one had thought of breaking out the road to the chapel, filled level with snow since the previous Sunday. Mr. Walker, always equal to the emergency, whipped up his plucky little span and led the way, closely followed by the groom and a long string of wedding guests.

The men, as was customary, took their seats on one side of the aisle, the women on the other. The bride, looking warm and pretty in a dress of red cashmere, bravely stood up without her shawl. The short service ended, all pressed forward to greet the new-married pair with a dignity and sobriety in pleasing contrast to the air of frolic and banter so characteristic of modern weddings.

Supper was served immediately in the adjoining community room—a well-cooked, appetizing meal prepared entirely by mission-trained women who had never been away to school. Six times the long table was cleared and quickly reset before all had eaten, and we saw loaves of excellent bread, apple pies, and doughnuts pressed upon departing guests. To be sure, it was customary at old-time Indian feasts for each to carry home whatever he was unable to consume on the spot. While still a novice, I once passed a large tray of cakes at an evening party and was startled to see the entire baking disappear in the folds of a capacious blanket!

We were consulted as naturally about family quarrels and neighborhood feuds as upon pleasanter occasions. A man of middle age had laid claim to his wife's young sister in accordance with an old custom. After she had run away from him once or twice, he applied to have her baptized, apparently as a guarantee of good behavior in the future. He was not accommodated.

Another young wife came to us in tears, imploring protection. Her husband, she said, had struck her, and she was afraid to go home. We pitied and took her in. The next night, after all was quiet, the repentant spouse could be heard tapping gently on the window pane and in soft accents begging her to return. She would not answer at first, but when we rose in the morning her couch was empty.

Our simple society was not entirely without class distinctions. Besides the recognized chiefs of various grades, whose prestige was well supported by government officials for their own purposes, there were families and individuals among us whose superior status was generally acknowledged. This might have been a holdover from the days of honors earned in intertribal war, or it might have marked a reputation for fine oratory, or for exceptional generosity. Distinction earned as a scout or salaried worker was beginning to be recognized. A few persons were described as "crazy," meaning wild or unreliable, others as "good-for-nothing." A thief was a marked man and despised accordingly. We seldom heard of a "bad" woman. Originally, I believe, the moral code was strict, the penalty for disobedience severe. I once heard an old man complain that "in the old days adultery was punished; now there is *only the law!*"

One of our nearest neighbors was reputed to be the only "old maid" in the tribe. The women told a romantic story to explain her strange refusal to wed. It seemed that a favorite brother had been accidentally shot and killed on a hunting trip by the man she had expected to marry. (Or possibly there was doubt as to its having been entirely an accident?) At all events, she took the tragedy so deeply to heart as to turn her against all mankind. She never appeared in church, but we exchanged many a friendly call with the grave-faced Miss Bird, now middle-aged, and the widowed sister called Dawn who shared her neat log-cabin home.

The two women's housekeeping was a model of its kind—the one room and large, bare yard swept perfectly clean, their blankets regularly aired, their clothing washed, and all their belongings in order. I can see them now, seated demurely with feet tucked under them (no woman sat cross-legged), on a neatly folded robe under the "leaf shadow," or rustic veranda, their hands busy with choice embroidery of store-bought beads or the more primitive dyed quills of the porcupine.

I had known her for more than a year when a change became noticeable. The slight, erect person had grown emaciated and the Bird could no longer stifle a hollow cough. When the quaint, kimonoed figured ceased to appear at our door with a piece of beadwork or a few eggs for sale, often carrying a pet raccoon like a baby on her back, the striped face peeping saucily over one shoulder, we went over often with a present of delicate food as an excuse for a chat. The sick woman asked no favors, made no complaints, and, like most of her race, met the near approach to death stoically. A new calico dress and the new moccasins with beaded soles for coffin wear hung in full view at the foot of her bed.

Early one wild March morning, I awoke to the high-pitched, sing-song wailing of the women—a sound of peculiar and unforgettable poignancy. On that same day, at sunset, I followed my little neighbor's long funeral procession, led by her favorite mount, up into the wild bluffs overlooking the village. The pony was laden with dress goods, handsomely beaded articles, and other possessions of the dead.

The plain pine box was lowered into a shallow grave and covered with a new folded tent. I inquired in a whisper why the coffin had been made so large. It seemed that they had dressed the slight form in several of her best gowns, wrapped it in fine blankets, and added as many ornaments as could possibly be worn. They had then placed about her in the box as many belongings as it would hold. The rest had been laid on the white pony for distribution among friends after the interment.

As soon as a little earth had been shoveled over the tent, a man selected for that duty placed a pistol to the ear of the beautiful horse, which uttered one piercing scream, almost human in its agony, as he fell at the feet of his mistress. This was the signal for a frantic storm of wailing and sobbing, mixed with a sort of chant in memory of the virtues of the dead woman. One woman bent over the partly exposed coffin of a relative who had slept there peacefully for many years, and with a fresh burst of crying took her shawl and spread it over him, remaining uncovered in the bitter wind to the close of the ceremony. The last act was a formal division of the goods among the large party of mourners.

Except that it was unusual to show so much honor to a woman, this was a typical Indian funeral. The time-hallowed custom of burying, burning, or giving away all one's possessions in the event of a death in the family was properly frowned upon by agents and missionaries. It did no one any good (unless it were a few greedy relatives) and added needlessly to the misery of the bereaved. The poor home was stripped, sometimes even deserted, leaving the ragged and destitute survivors practically objects of charity. I recall that real courage was shown by one young mother in our village who had lately been baptized. Defying the slurs of her neighbors, she brought her dead baby to us to be robed and coffined in white for Christian burial, only pleading for permission to leave one loved toy in the cold little hand.

The ancient usage of tree-burial had not long been obsolete at this period. The fear of ghosts was all but universal. To mention the name of the dead or to pass near his last resting place was to invite some mysterious doom. No one but ourselves would consider keeping a body in the house overnight. We tried to combat this superstition by many kind offices and by leading our little flock to decorate the graves in the Christian burying ground with wreaths of wild flowers on each Memorial Day.

The solemn ritual of the "Ghost Lodge" had all but disappeared, and it was my privilege to attend as spectator on one of the last—perhaps the very last—of these occasions. I was the sole representative of my race among a great crowd of Dakotas garbed in their colorful best. Many were wailing musically or chanting antiphonally a litany of praise. Some publicly slashed their arms and legs and pulled out their own hair by handfuls—surely an extreme expression of grief for one who had been under the sod more than two years!

After the formal mourning and the burial of the "ghost" or sacred relics, came gift giving on a scale of unusual magnificence and last the feast, all of old-time dainties. There were great kettles of *teepsinna*, or

Indian turnips (the *pomme blanche* of the French), others of hulled corn softened with lye and cooked like coarse hominy, and *wasna*, which is pounded sun-dried meat mixed with pounded and dried cherries. Each guest brought his own dish and spoon, and men and women ate standing about in separate groups. I noticed that even the bails of the pots and the handles of the new tin dippers used in serving were gaily ornamented with bands and tassels of dyed cornhusk.

RED MEN "ON RELIEF"

THE CHIEF POPULAR AMUSEMENT IN OUR DAY
was the Omaha, or grass, dance—a kind of masque
performed by young men attired mainly in paint of
gorgeous hues with elaborate feather headdresses
and ornaments of shells, bells, and bears' claws.
These striking figures vividly pantomimed the brave
deeds of old. Fifty years ago, fresh from my first
glimpse of the exotic spectacle, I described it thus:

> The throbs of the dance-drum measure the hot, breathless
> silence. Against a background of sunburnt grass and dazzling
> sky assemble groups of gazers. The step is indescribable—it is
> as if the dancers were treading on hot iron or pointed knives,
> so delicately do they touch the sod and so fantastically bend
> their supple bodies in perfect time with the singing of the old
> men. The music lasts for a few minutes, stops abruptly and all
> seat themselves. After a brief interval it begins again, and
> perhaps two men rise, or it may be twenty, to repeat in-
> definitely the series of short turns that lend a dramatic effect
> to the performance.

An Italian count, traveling over the prairies a
century ago, saw this same dance as "merely poses,

grotesque and rather ugly. . . . You would have said the devil had entered into their bodies."[1]

Women took no part in the Omaha except as spectators and their own dance was by comparison uninteresting. It consisted of a rhythmic rising on the toes and sinking back again, without moving appreciably from the original position. Their dress was, as always, completely unrevealing, though brightly colored, and their attitudes modest. We were expected to frown upon all "heathen spectacles," but could not help knowing that the modern round dance in which men and women publicly embrace was a shocking thing in the eyes of our ceremonious Dakotas.

About once a month the "beef issue" formed a good excuse for a general assemblage and the ensuing festival. At the larger agencies (but not Lower Brulé), beef was issued "on the hoof." As each excited animal was released from the corral, a crier with stentorian voice named the heads of families to whom the meat was assigned. A mob of a hundred or more Indians, each mounted on his best pony, and armed with a repeating rifle, surrounded the exit. Wild, long-horned Texas cattle galloped madly over the open prairie, each one closely followed by several yelling horsemen. Shots rang out, and screams of exultation were mingled with howls of contemptuous laughter when someone's aim was bad. Dead and dying beasts lay all about. Carcasses were butchered while yet warm by the women and old men. Soon blue curls of smoke began to steal upward from frugal small fires and hungry families to gather about the teasing fragrance of boiling meat. Liver and other tidbits were eaten raw while mothers prepared

1. Count Francesco Arese, *A Trip to the Prairies and the Interior of North America*, trans. Andrew Evans (New York: Harbor Press, 1934), p. 88.

portions for the pot. The greater part was sliced in thin strips to be dried in the open air—their only means of preservation until the next Issue Day.

Once every year at that time, and always in severe winter weather, came the *wakpamni*, or annual distribution of clothing.

"I have seen thirteen issues, and I have never known *wakpamni* week to pass without a severe cold snap, or a snowstorm," observed Mrs. Walker on the morning of the second of December 1887. (The Treaty of 1868 had stipulated that it must occur no later than August first!)

"This is perhaps the busiest week of the year at an Indian agency," I wrote to *The Christian Union*. "The agent, sub-agent, and clerks, with the army inspector, Captain Bean, whose duty it is to superintend the issue and certify its correctness, have burned the midnight oil over complicated rows of figures. Now comes the actual distribution, demanding the services of every available person in the place, from blacksmith to lady missionary.

"The people are assembling from all parts of the reservation, whole families of them—men, women, children, ponies, dogs. Some have come a two-days journey. They are camping down in the timber, the tipis cunningly concealed in the underbrush. A pair of parti-colored ponies are pulling locks of hay from a bright green wagon box, outside the artistically smoke-colored cone of the Dakota lodge. An old crone bends over a newly slain dog, preparing him for the evening meal. Men are smoking; women tending babies, or watching the soup kettle, or weaving brilliantly tinted porcupine quills into a pattern on a pair of moccasins. They are a sociable, kindly, hospitable, unsuspicious folk.

"The next morning finds us gathered in a big, bare structure, cold as a barn, with a round-bellied wood stove in the middle doing its little utmost. Up and down the whitewashed walls are ranged in orderly piles the dark blue blankets, the gay calico quilts, the bolts of flannel, linsey, gingham, sheeting, the shirts and suits, hats and shoes each year doled out to these wards of the nation. Men of every shade of complexion, in buffalo coats, enormous mufflers, and felt boots, are sitting or standing in easy attitudes about the red-hot stove. A high counter shuts off a narrow space at one end of the long room. The issue clerk bends over the counter with a big book open before him and begins to call off the names in order. His assistants take their places before their respective piles. The doors are guarded by tall Indian police.

"The head chief, Iron Nation, is first named by the clerk and his name is repeated in Dakota by the interpreter, who stands beside him. The captain of police unbolts the door and sends out a ringing call. The old man comes forward with what dignity he can muster and touches the pencil which signs the receipt. Each article due him is then named in turn and the person who has it in charge must repeat the call in a loud sing-song.

" 'ONE AND A HALF BLANKETS! One and a half blankets!' echoes from the far end of the room. 'ONE FLANNEL SHIRT—MEN'S! One flannel shirt—men's! ONE BOY—DUCK! One boy—duck! FOURTEEN SHEETING! Fourteen sheeting! TWENTY-FIVE BUTTONS! Twenty-five buttons!'—and so on and so on. Boys run to and fro with each article as named, and by the time the end of the list is reached, a huge bundle is made up on the counter. The blanket, upon which everything else is deposited, is gathered by the four corners and lifted or dragged out, after which exit Iron Nation and enter the next on the roll.

"We, the lady missionary and the day school teacher, enthroned upon high stools to the left of the counter, preside over the pins and buttons, commanding the best view in the room of the odd, grotesque, pathetic parade. The old men and maidens come in for their shares. Now and then a small child draws for the family. Old Man Bear is announced—and a handsome boy of perhaps ten, whose uncombed head can just be seen above the counter, leans a-tiptoe to touch the pen, with a half-scared, half-pleased expression. A couple have quarreled overnight and ask to have their goods divided and issued to them separately. Occasionally, someone is reported sick, absent, or (in one case) asleep, and an uncle or son-in-law or other relative appears to draw his annuity for him, which (after being questioned and identified) he is usually permitted to do.

"Now and then a recipient of Uncle Sam's indiscriminate bounty returns to request, with emphatic gestures, a larger coat or a number nine shoe. It is inseparable from the system that misfits should occur, and that many should get things they do not want.

"How much do the Indians receive on an average? It looks like a good deal when the allotted portion of a large family is heaped up before your eyes. The men get a shoddy blanket apiece, the women a cheap quilt. Each man is issued a full suit of clothes, hat, and boots; each woman six or eight yards of linsey for a dress, some flannel, gingham, unbleached cotton, a shawl, and a few sundries. Yet so poor is the quality that the total cost to the government is only about ten dollars, according to the agent's estimate.

[62]

"Annuities are not free gifts, but are issued in accordance with treaty stipulations in part payment for land. It has often been asked: Why not make instead small annual or monthly payments in cash to heads of families, thus helping to increase self-respect and teach them the use of money?

"Most of us here approve that plan. It is opposed by some who argue that Indians would waste or gamble away their cash annuities; also that they could not buy useful articles as cheaply as can the government at wholesale prices, perhaps forgetting that the whole cost of purchasing, transporting, and issuing these bulky supplies ought to be added to the share of the Sioux. (But what would become of the contractor's profit, to say nothing of possible official graft?)

"I dislike to see my friends file in, one by one, seize and carry off their booty! To see an educated youth touch the pencil with shamefaced air! Dreariest of all is the picture framed for us at intervals in the open doorway—a semicircle of women, many with babies in their arms, sitting on the frozen ground in a whirl of falling snowflakes, waiting patiently for their turn."

I came to understand better after a time that most of these goods were nearly worthless and a burden to the recipients, who often threw them away or sold them for whatever they could get. The poor white settler on the borders of the reservation could buy a suit of clothes for a dollar, shoes for a quarter, flannel for ten cents a yard while the annuities lasted.

July and August were vacation months. My colleague took the train for the East as soon as school was out. She urged me to come, too, but I protested that I couldn't afford the trip. My pay was only six hundred a year. She suggested that I ask the bank in Chamberlain to advance my next two months' salary, and in that way I contrived to finance a summer at home. After the first year I spent my holidays in travel over the Great Sioux Reservation, which then covered almost thirty thousand square miles, gradually familiarizing myself with its main features and the personnel of the six separate agencies.

I bought an Indian pony for twenty dollars and had a small tent made. So equipped, I was ready to join a family party who might be moving in the desired direction, for they were a people fond of visiting and often on the road. Once, I met with earnest remonstrance from the Indian agent at Rosebud, a hundred miles west of White River. The people with whom I had journeyed so far were going no farther. I made a few inquiries and arranged with a family of total strangers to carry me on to my destination, another hundred and fifty miles across the sagebrush prairies. This meant at least four nights on the road.

The gray-haired official, paternal and authoritative in manner, was frankly shocked by my temerity. I assured him that I was perfectly safe and entirely happy with my Dakota friends, having coldly declined the invitation of a young white employee to accompany him in his buggy. However, Major [L. F.] Spencer insisted, notwithstanding my protests, on supplying me with a guard of honor in the persons of two fine-looking, six-foot native police, uniformed, armed, and mounted!

We proceeded very agreeably over the vast open spaces—a slow-moving, white-topped wagon and trio of equestrians conversing merrily by the way, for by this time I spoke the vernacular with ease. We took our meals together as one family. At night I occupied

[64]

my solitary tipi and the Rosebud party their own, while my gallant protectors slept under the stars.

One night there were no stars and presently rain began to fall heavily. I was aroused by a hail from the neighboring tent.

"If you could give two of us room in your lodge," cried a woman's voice, "our soldier friends could shelter here. They are getting very wet."

"*Chinto!* Why, of course!" I responded, wishing that I had thought of it first. Quietly, in the pitch darkness the change was made. I did not know who shared my apartment and awoke in the morning to find myself alone as usual.

Later on, I often spent the night in a well-filled tipi, entirely surrounded by men, women, children, and dogs, all without the slightest self-consciousness. The etiquette of the tipi is strict. Each person has his bed, which is also his seat by day—mine being always the seat of honor at the back of the lodge, opposite the entrance. The privacy of each is inviolable, and no Dakota would think of transgressing, even by a look, that invisible barrier. If men were present, they stayed outside in the evening until the women had retired, afterward entering noiselessly, each to his own place. Again, in the early morning, they considerately disappeared while we made our toilets for the day. Like the native women, I did not undress completely—merely took off my shoes, loosened my garments, and let down my hair.

Solicitous white friends urged me never to travel with Indians unarmed. They were poor psychologists and poorer realists. A revolver in my baggage would only have served to advertise lack of trust in my companions—and in the fact that I did trust them completely lay my sole and sufficient guarantee of safety.

Perhaps I should confess that I never became entirely reconciled to the dogs. They had fleas; they whined or grunted from time to time; they preferred to sleep on our feet; and if I should chance to sleep late, they might even steal my breakfast!

Arrived at Pine Ridge, I paid off the driver of the wagon with a five-dollar bill and purchased two of the best pocketknives at the trader's store as a farewell present to my escort. Here, I was for a few days the guest of the young, college-bred rector, Charles Smith Cook, and his charming wife. Mr. Cook was the son of a Sioux woman and an army officer, who had been adopted and thoroughly educated by one of the early missionaries. He was both an able and a singularly attractive man, with winning manners and a smile of great sweetness. Jessie Wells Cook, member of a New England family, a college graduate and skilled musician, became my intimate friend. The young couple had been burned out almost as soon as they reached their new home, losing wedding gifts and everything they owned except the clothes they stood in. Such are the common vicissitudes of frontier life, where houses are flimsily built and fire protection lacking. However, a new and better rectory had been built and furnished, and I found them snugly established there in the summer of 1888.

It may seem strange that one so sure of her true vocation as I have been ever since I was twelve or fourteen years old could be entirely content with the life and work I have tried to describe. However, I was more than content—for most of the time I was enthusiastically happy. I never stopped writing, but my writing was wholly secondary to my work for Indians and tributary to it. It was done at odd moments, or late at night, in longhand and little, if at all, revised. Religious and educational journals of the day printed everything I cared to send them, descriptive, didactic, or in fictional form—rarely in verse. The reason for this must have been that Indians were a live issue then. I have counted over twenty different newspapers and magazines to which I was a contributor in the eighties and nineties. I can't remember a time when I wouldn't "rather write than eat," and while literary ambition was for many years entirely subordinated to "the cause" (and later to my family), the notion still stayed unreasonably in the back of my head that some day I might write a book that would live.

INDIANS ARE PEOPLE!

THE BETTER WE CAME TO KNOW OUR NEW neighbors, the more unreal appeared the popular emphasis upon racial traits. Such characteristics as most of them seemed to possess in common were obviously the result of a segregated and narrowly framed culture. Aside from these, we found all varieties of human nature, good, bad, and indifferent, among two or three hundred "wild" blanket Indians.

On the very day that school opened for the first time, a tall, fine-looking stranger appeared from a neighboring camp on the other side of the White, or "Smoking Earth," River. He had walked three miles on that bitter January day, holding two small boys by either grimy hand—little fellows in suits of *wakpamni* several sizes too big, with uncombed elf-locks and what looked like the accumulated dirt of weeks on their hands and faces. Both were blue with cold and evidently frightened out of their wits.

Our friend of the Roman nose, hawk's eyes, and caressing voice introduced himself as the Swallow—a name appropriate according to native ideas, but which had been grotesquely translated into English as Little Forked Tail. He presented his sons with parental pride, quite unconscious of their absurd appearance. Both, he informed us without embarrassment, were eight years old, but they were not twins. They had different mothers. He wished both sons to be educated and to "become like white men."

Promising to bring them to school every day, Little Forked Tail released the youngsters with a parting admonition and settled himself in a back seat to observe their progress in acquiring an education. Our first step in that direction was to lead them to the washroom and introduce them to some much needed soap and water. It was seen at once that the smaller and slighter of the two was sadly disfigured by a harelip. At the end of the morning session, their father was courteously invited to give them a full bath at home and to cut their hair, to which strange request he assented without demur.

Faithfully persisting in his self-imposed task, he continued to escort the boys to school in all weather, occasionally relieved by one of his wives, who were sisters—two gaunt, silent women. For a few weeks the White River could be crossed on the ice, but after it broke up early in March one could only leap perilously from one floating block to the next or wade waist-deep in the icy flood, carrying one child at a time. The two "Little Tails," as they inevitably came to be called, were, not unreasonably, afraid to attempt it alone. Their father usually left them with us and went about his business, returning in time to take them home in the late afternoon, but either mother would sit all day on the floor in an inconspicuous corner, beading a pair of moccasins with stiffened fingers, never asking favors of any kind, and at the close of school returning as she came.

The boy with the harelip, whom we named Henry, was painfully conscious of his deformity, and no wonder. It hindered articulation and in every way seriously interfered with his development. Could not something be done? We consulted the agency doctor and found him willing to operate. The case was put fairly before Little Forked Tail, who gave a reluctant consent—provided the boy and his mother were willing. Henry cried bitterly, heart-brokenly; and no argument, no appeal availed with the superstitious Dakota woman. One saw that in her simple mind it was not well to meddle with mysteries. So the child continued in school, learning little besides habits of neatness, order, and obedience. He could write but was afraid to try to speak and seemed mainly anxious to keep out of sight.

Even more unfortunate, if possible, was the reflex effect of Henry's handicap upon William's disposition. He thrust himself forward in proportion as his brother held back, and seemed every day more selfish, vain, and arrogant. A handsome little fellow, especially when in a rage; his nostrils dilated, the bold eyes glittered, and the well-cut features betrayed a pride and determination beyond his years. He learned quickly but was impatient of control. His father never punished him—few Indian fathers do— but in his gentle way he upheld our authority and we could not but respect his conscientious efforts to treat his sons with strict impartiality.

Our friend was plainly disappointed to discover that an education was not to be achieved in a few short months. However, he never noticeably faltered in his purpose, nor for a moment relaxed his chivalrous courtesy toward his boys' teachers.

After the next distribution of annuity goods he reported with his usual composure that a mistake had been made. Only one boy's suit had been issued to him. This, of course, had been instantly claimed by William, and little Henry, left out in the cold, had cried all night and in the morning refused to eat or come to school. Only William appeared, glowing and exultant, in the coarse new clothes.

We had, fortunately, several extra suits at our disposal, and the smallest of these was handed over at once, with a gaily bordered handkerchief tucked into a pocket by way of consolation for Henry's disappointment. Next day, the father came alone with further explanations. The spoiled favorite of fortune, resenting a gift in which he had no share, had torn the innocent handkerchief to bits with his teeth. He was sulking in his tent and the despoiled little brother was again in tears!

Not long after this, word came of Henry's illness and we looked him up at once. We found the little fellow lying in a half stupor on a pile of unsavory quilts in the close room where the whole family lived, ate, and slept. It was evident that he didn't care about getting well. It was enough to know that for the moment, at least, somebody put him first. When all was over, perhaps no one but the mother really mourned Henry. We felt that it was better for his brother to have no one at hand to feed his inordinate sense of superiority.

Little Forked Tail had begun almost at once to attend our Sunday services at White River. He had a logical mind, able to grasp the richer values of the new teaching, as compared with a vague and fearful nature worship. Having set his face firmly toward the future, he wished now to join the church.

But there was still one all but insurmountable obstacle. He had three wives. The mothers of his two sons were no longer young or pleasing, while the third wife was a pretty, young girl. He could not bear to give her up. At the same time, his strong sense of justice would not permit him to choose her, discarding the women who had served him faithfully for years.

Time passed and our neighbor's problems were partially solved for him. The young wife went into a decline; she lost flesh steadily; she developed an obstinate cough. We were forced to realize that she was dying.

No husband could have been more devoted. He lavished time and means upon her, to the neglect of all other duties, gave his ponies one by one to the medicine man to pay for his herbs and incantations, even sold his cows to buy her canned fruit and other delicacies. We did not see him for some time after her death, but it had helped him to make up his mind. Accepting the situation, he presently made provision for his second wife and was legally married to the mother of his remaining son. Both united with the church and our friend became a strong and reasonably consistent Christian.

It was told of him that on one occasion he had been persuaded by some old friends to enter again the sweat lodge, or vapor bath, on the plea that it was no religious ceremony this time, but solely for health and cleanliness. However, habits are strong and soon the ancient songs began to issue amid clouds of steam from the lips of the bathers.

"Let the Dakotas remember their own gods!" exclaimed one, "and let each man sing to the god he worships!"

The new convert listened aghast to what now seemed to him the impious and diabolic invocations that followed. Recovering courage, he struck up "Jesus, Lover of My Soul" in the native dialect. The effect was instantaneous. Within half a minute the place was cleared and the Christian worshiper found himself alone.

One Shunkaska, or White Dog, a wild youth dressed in a sheet, divided his time between dancing, horse racing, gambling with plumstones, and teasing the girls. A native missionary suddenly opened school in a log cabin nearby. For a few months this disciple of the Reverend John Williamson[1] gathered together a handful of people of all ages and both sexes with the simple aim of teaching them to read the Scriptures in their own tongue.

Every morning a rag of white fluttered from the cabin roof to indicate that school was open. The pupils came and went at their pleasure with little attempt at order or discipline. They did learn something, nevertheless. White Dog, who had dropped in one day out of sheer curiosity, became faithful in attendance. He readily mastered the new art and was soon an earnest student of the Dakota Bible—his teacher's parting gift.

One day there appeared at our door a young man of serious and thoughtful aspect, neatly if shabbily attired in citizens' clothes. He said little but a pair of singularly bright, appealing eyes spoke for him. I learned that Peter was now a trained lay worker in the Presbyterian church, living alone, and report said irreproachable in conduct. He began to haunt our house, always modest and respectful, hungrily gleaning a few words in English and picking up chance bits of information wherever he might. Small refinements of dress and manners were assimilated with unusual quickness.

Peter addressed prayer meetings with a moving eloquence, as I discovered for myself after I had

---

1. John P. Williamson (1835–1917) was a Presbyterian missionary at the Yankton agency.

sufficiently mastered the Dakota language to appre-
ciate the finer touches. His solitary studies had borne
fruit in an original and often suggestive interpretation of a hackneyed passage. His favorite hymn,
literally translated "Jesus, I my cross have tak-
en . . . ," rang out with a poignant sincerity after his
application to enter Hampton had been denied because of health. This disappointment no doubt has-
tened his end, which came—of tuberculosis—before
the age of thirty.

One John, significantly nicknamed Wamanon, or
Thief, surprised and attracted us at the outset by an
unusual display of energy and promptness. The first
time he came, his not inconsiderable weight caused a
kitchen chair to groan ominously. Instantly rising, he
picked it up, examined it with care, and found a loose
round. With hardly a word he looked about for glue,
found it, carried the chair outside, and mended it
neatly. From that day on, he seemed to take us under
his wing and for several months made himself generally useful about the mission. After a few days, he
brought his rather harum-scarum wife, whom we
called Kate, and introduced her into the sewing
circle. Both applied for baptism and membership in
the church.

It was apparent that neither John nor Kate had a
good name in the village. We rather resented the fact
but were disconcerted to learn that both had once
been received into the Congregational fold and
proved conspicuous backsliders. However, we were
more than willing to give them a second chance. Mr.
Walker took the same view and put them on six
months' probation, after which they were not to be
rebaptized, but confirmed by the Bishop and properly married.

So far as we knew, their behavior was exemplary up to the very day set for the two important ceremonies. The Bishop came; the bell was rung; the congregation assembled—but where were John and Kate? Someone was sent for the laggards and returned to report their cabin vacant. The birds had flown.

My frequent trips over the reservation familiarized me with a variety of frontier types. I recall clearly a tall, stooped figure hurrying out into the October twilight to welcome our party to a remote mission station. This man with the grizzled beard, honest blue eyes, and strong Teutonic accent was a man with a history. Its strange romance was in my thoughts as I followed him into the clean, bare room where the Sioux wife, with a baby in her arms, kept humbly in the background, while the pretty eldest daughter, who had been away to school, bashfully did the honors of the plentifully spread table. A flock of youngsters of all ages displayed odd but pleasing combinations of blue eyes and coal-black locks or fair hair with marked Indian features.

The Bishop had told me that this Schmidt was born in Germany about fifty years earlier. A studious youth of religious turn of mind, he wanted to study for the ministry and go as a missionary to darkest Africa. Upon his father's death he was left to the guardianship of a well-to-do uncle, who flatly refused to sanction any such fantastic plan. Finding his nephew obstinate, he had him drafted into the army. Unable to bear that life, the boy presently deserted and ran away—to America.

Landing on these shores without money or friends, he sank into the social depths; drifted gradually westward; associated with cowboys, trappers, and

Indians. After figuring in many a rash adventure and wild carouse, he ended by taking a Dakota woman to wife.

In those days the Rosebud, or Spotted Tail, agency looked weird and desolate enough, flung casually, as it were, into a devil's dance of barren little hills. You descended abruptly upon it, almost as if alighting on the roofs of the few squalid houses. The chapel, with log parsonage close by, perched atop a sandy eminence. There was a headlong descent, another steep pitch, and a row of government buildings painted a gloomy chocolate. (They had originally been white, but the unrelieved glare of the intense sun on white paint had proved intolerable.) Some log huts, with here and there a clump of snowy tipis like great bell-shaped flowers, completed the landscape.

During the first struggling days of the Episcopal mission, after the assassination of the head chief, Spotted Tail, Schmidt happened to ride into the agency while the newly hung church bell smote powerfully the oppressively still air of the high plains.[2] Learning that one of his former comrades was about to be carried to the grave, he could do no less than follow. The solemn words of the prayer book brought back old associations with overwhelming force and he fled from them into the wilderness.

Returning weeks later from a mad gallop without purpose or goal, again he heard the church bell ringing. Schmidt had lost count of the days, but actually it was Sunday morning. The man angrily pulled on the bridle, determined to ride away, but found himself instead approaching the plain gothic chapel atop the sandy butte. When he reached it the

---

2. Spotted Tail, chief of the Brulé Sioux, was shot by a fellow tribesman near the Rosebud agency in August 1881.

bell had ceased, and through the open windows there floated the soft, persuasive air of a familiar hymn.

Schmidt threw himself from his horse and came closer, impelled by something stronger than his own will. Next instant, he had entered the church.

He did not see what he had expected. No robed clergyman stood before him. A handful of men and women and children were grouped about a parlor organ. A woman of the sort he had once known turned toward the newcomer with a smile and a kind word, making of this day one never to be forgotten. The hard-working missionary had been suddenly called to a distant station and his devoted wife had summoned the people for a simple service of prayer and praise.

Two months later, the former outlaw was installed as sexton, and after a year of probation, he was permitted to go out as catechist into a heathen camp, there to teach, exhort, and comfort his adopted people.

A LIVING OFF THE LAND

"THOSE LAZY, DIRTY, GOOD-FOR-NOTHING Sioux!" Such was the cry of the ambitious speculator in town lots, the western politician, the industrious and land-hungry immigrant. "They don't need all that land. Everybody knows that Injuns won't work!"

In the words of Dr. Fred Riggs, a missionary of the third generation, brought up among these people, the Sioux had, in fact, plenty of energy and initiative—otherwise they could not have survived under the hard conditions of primitive life.[1] Theirs was an incessant, hand-to-hand struggle against hunger and cold, wild beasts, and lurking enemies.

What motive was there for regular, persistent labor under the new dispensation? We exterminated the buffalo which originally furnished them with a livelihood, confined them to a limited range of the least

---

1. Frederick B. Riggs, the son of Alfred Riggs and grandson of Stephen Return Riggs—both Congregational missionaries to the Sioux—served as the superintendent of the Santee Normal Training School, on the Santee Reservation, from 1916 to 1933.

desirable part of their territory (for the purpose of cultivation), and doled out just enough monotonous food and shoddy clothing to keep them alive. It was proposed gradually to transform nomadic hunters into farmers, a difficult but by no means an impossible feat. (Some tribes have long been successful agriculturists.) Money was appropriated by Congress to buy seed, implements, and fence wire, and to employ an instructor in farming at every agency. Let us see just how the plan worked in the Dakota of the eighteen eighties.

The "assistant farmer" of that day, not unlike the average office-holder before civil service reform, was usually a political henchman or needy favorite of some man higher up. Such posts were poorly paid and regarded as desirable mainly because of opportunities for private pickings. "We're none of us here for our health" was the common and significant jest. Many farmers, to my personal knowledge, devoted most of their time to hauling water, cutting ice, cultivating small vegetable gardens, and doing other chores for the agent. When they did undertake to instruct an Indian, their ignorance was sometimes laughable. I heard of one who directed his neophytes to cut turnips in pieces and plant them in hills!

Plowing in South Dakota may be begun as early as February or March. Let us suppose that one Little Bull, seeing nothing for it but to walk henceforth in the white man's road, has made up his mind to put in a crop. The first step is to join a crude local Grange which meets from time to time during the winter, for the enjoyment of much long-winded debate and a substantial supper.

Having none of his own, he applies to the assistant farmer for the use of a plow. One is assigned to him for a given period—perhaps ten days. When the preordained date arrives (provided it doesn't rain, that Little Bull isn't sick, and that the farmer hasn't forgotten and let another man have the plow), the would-be planter stands before his cabin door and utters a musical halloo which may be heard at a distance of at least half a mile. This is the regular way of issuing a general invitation and in this case is understood to mean that the caller bids his fellow Grangers to a plowing bee.

In the course of the morning several pony teams appear and cut a shallow, uneven furrow around the selected piece of ground. The tough prairie sod and the heavy breaking-plow form a combination that is almost too much for these light, unseasoned ponies, used to "rustling" pasture for themselves and innocent of the taste of grain. The slenderly muscled bodies of the amateur farmers are better suited to spurts of intense effort than to continuous toil. Their bright-hued shirt-tails and long black hair float on the stiff breeze as they run and leap and almost dance behind the plow. The ponies sweat and strain, jerk and tug desperately; the much mended harness often gives way; and Little Bull is fortunate indeed if the plow does not break—perhaps forty miles from a blacksmith shop. At the end of every round, all the men sit down in a ring and the inevitable long red pipe is passed from hand to hand.

By the time the field is plowed—or half plowed more likely—it is time to eat. The wives have been busy, too. They appear on the scene at noon by the sun, laden with steaming coffee pots, kettles of boiled beef, and huge piles of fried bread, each round the size of a dinner plate. Again the circle is formed, this time including many who have been no more than interested spectators at the morning's labor.

The farmer has duly applied for enough grain to plant his field. He may have asked for a few potatoes with seed of melons, squashes, and other vegetables. He is lucky if he gets half as much as he wants of any of these. The agent's estimates, none too liberal to begin with, have been severely pruned in Washington, in the interest of "economy." Little Bull cannot understand why a great and rich nation should invite him into partnership and afterward fall down on its part of the bargain.

The native fertility of our Dakota soil was then untapped, but sufficient rainfall was to be expected no more than one year in three. Careless fencing led to much destruction by horses and cattle. Necessary trips to the agency after supplies and long visits to relatives in other jurisdictions seriously interfered with proper cultivation of corn. Occasionally a fine crop of wheat was lost for lack of timely help in threshing and marketing the grain, with the nearest gristmill fifty to a hundred miles away, on the other side of the great river. At long intervals, separated by miles of crisp buffalo grass or silvery sage, prickly white poppies, and blazing wild sunflowers, cramped cornfields choked with weeds marked the unequal fight.

It was sometimes urged that the government buy the Indian's surplus produce on the spot for distribution, instead of importing it. This seemed a common-sense plan to all except contractors and others interested in supplying the Indian Service. The Sioux could easily have grown all their own beef and probably their flour or cornmeal as well. Yet even the cash business of freighting supplies from the nearest railroad station was usually given to white men! Agent McGillycuddy at Pine Ridge was one of the first to insist that the Sioux should have it. This reform was inaugurated in 1878, under Secretary [of the Interior Carl] Schurz, and the Oglalas alone were

[81]

said to have earned forty-five thousand dollars in one year by freighting.

A double error has been made through the years in assuming that red men are incompetents—hardly men at all, in fact—and in building up a vested right among white men to work they might far better have done for themselves. As communities they have been practically without money and so unable to buy the product of one another's labor. In my day, there were among them no blacksmiths, carpenters, or shoemakers whose services could be purchased. Although young men were already being taught these trades in eastern schools, one who attempted to practice them at home must starve for lack of custom. So, probably, would the enterprising "returned student" who managed to open a small store, breaking the monopoly of the licensed trader, whose exorbitant prices were a standing grievance. His technique was to hold his customers by keeping them continuously in debt.

The limited number of salaried positions open to Indians in government employ was no real solution, although ability to secure one of these posts was, and still is, practically the only chance to earn a decent living on the reservation. The man with a regular pay check, however small, was handicapped by incessant demands upon his hospitality, an obligation impossible to evade under tribal custom. That there has been little gain in these respects in the past half century is indicated by the most recent official survey, which states that "no opportunity exists within the home area for wage employment, except of a temporary nature in emergency government agencies."

The Sioux naturally tended to huddle in groups along the creeks and river bottoms, where shade, water, and some fuel might be had, rather than to "scatter out" on the open prairie, as required under the "land in severalty" system.[2] It was hard to give up the prized social life of a small neighborhood for an isolated claim and even harder to travel eighty or a hundred miles once every fortnight after rations, with frequent breakdowns of wagons and harnesses on the road. Whenever a new "count" was ordered or "*wakpamni* week" came around in the dead of winter, it was customary to take the entire family to camp in tents, leaving pigs and poultry, if any, to their fate. Even today, I am told, the home ranch is similarly neglected for a chance of a few weeks' work on the CCC or for the doubtful amusements of a rodeo!

But (you may ask) wasn't it known fifty years ago that most of the Great Sioux Reservation was fit only for grazing and much of it "bad lands" fit for nothing at all? A glance at the record proves that the well-informed knew then, as well as we know now, that the Sioux could never expect to support themselves by agriculture. Without artificial irrigation, it is still only in exceptional years that a crop can be raised. Indeed, the water table has fallen and droughts are growing more severe, as everyone realizes. Many of the white settlers who followed the Sioux with high hopes and industrious habits have since abandoned their claims. A general depopulation of that part of the country is not at all impossible. Deep tillage, green manuring, and fallowing have all been tried and found, in the main, unprofitable.

In a word, this is and always has been a cattle country. Not isolated quarter-sections of treeless and waterless prairie, but cooperative herds or individually owned cattle pastured on common land,

---

2. The 1887 General Allotment Act (commonly called the Dawes Act after its sponsor, Senator Henry L. Dawes) authorized the President to proceed with the allotment of Indian reservations in severalty.

might have solved the problem for those Dakotas who chose to stay where they were. I knew white men married to Sioux women who amassed a competence in this way. The standard excuse for discouraging so natural a trend was that herding, as a way of life, was too much like the old hunting economy! It could, however, have been combined with ownership of a small, well-watered homestead and garden spot, as was done by the better class of "squaw men."

OPENING THE RESERVATION

FIFTY YEARS AGO A GIFTED, LOVABLE, SELF-RELI-
ant people stood at the crisis of their fate. The old
way of life was hopelessly destroyed and their more
far-seeing leaders ready and eager to advance into a
new world. They might still have preferred their
own, if given a choice, but since there was no choice,
they wanted to advance much faster than we would
let them. The hour had struck for a swift transition to
another pattern of life altogether, before their self-
respect had been undermined and their courage exhausted. Having lived at the heart of the issue for
half a century, I deeply regret the folly of holding the
tribes together in compact masses and teaching them
dependence upon the federal government. It has,
quite unnecessarily, kept the majority of Indians
children and wards to this day.

Says a man proud of his Sioux heritage and background and at the same time adequate to present-day
demands: "There is plenty of evidence to prove that

one generation is more than sufficient to civilize Indians, provided they have the same opportunities given ordinary citizens. The reservation system and department policy is to blame for keeping them back."

Notwithstanding the aridity of the short-grass plains and the extensive "bad lands" where nothing would grow, there was strong pressure for opening the Sioux reservation in the eighteen-eighties. The drive at that time was probably initiated by the railroads and kept alive by speculators in town sites and by the local press.

My spirited little partner, Laura Tileston, decided to rejoin her mother in the summer of 1888. The Bishop was good enough to consult me in the matter of a successor. In default of my sister Dora, who declined the position, an unmarried sister of my mother's came that fall to live with me and carry on the work of the White River mission. After superintending some additions to our shanty, I spent most of that summer in cross-country travel, and had not long returned from my visit to the Cooks at Pine Ridge, when the Pratt Commission reached Lower Brulé.

This commission, appointed for the purpose of securing the signatures of three-quarters of the adult males to the so-called "Sioux bill," was headed by Captain Richard H. Pratt, founder and principal of the famous Carlisle School. His colleagues were Judge [John V.] Wright of Tennessee and an Episcopal missionary, the Reverend Mr. [William J.] Cleveland, known as the Long Pine. The new treaty—for such it was in substance, though not in name—provided for the sale of one-third to one-half the reservation to the government, after which it was to be thrown open to settlement. For each band it meant a separate and much reduced territory, while the Lower Brulés were to be moved bodily some forty miles up the river. Practically all government employees worked for the bill and it was supported by the Episcopal church as well. We understood, however, that the chiefs were opposed and that Standing Rock and Cheyenne River had been approached before us and had refused to sign.

Nearly every man, woman, and child in the tribe was on hand when the council opened under a large awning in front of our agency. The officials, seated in chairs, faced concentric rows of eager listeners, sitting, standing, and on horseback. The matter was of sufficient general interest to rate front-page dispatches, even editorials in the New York papers. School was out of the question, and I set about reporting the discussions for *The Independent* from the point of view of the Sioux, whose language and sentiments were by this time thoroughly familiar. It gave me a real "kick," I confess, to follow their speeches in the vernacular without waiting for a tedious interpretation, in which some of the characteristic touches were inevitably lost.

The question of what to do with the Indians was not, even then, of vital importance to the country at large, and in these days possesses little more than academic interest—except to themselves. The Sioux were not slow to grasp the far-reaching implications of this new offer, urged upon them only twenty years after they had been promised undisputed possession of an empire "as long as grass grows and water runs." They were divided upon the wisdom of accepting it, but few, if any, were persuaded by the conventional gestures and protestations of generosity into the belief that it had been mainly conceived for their benefit.

One group disclaimed all faith in the honor of the white man—"all bald heads are liars!"—avowed a decided preference for ancestral customs, and declined to part with another acre upon any terms. Another party were willing to bargain, but intended to take their own time about it. The body of mixed-bloods and men of better mental calibre or a smattering of education perceived clearly that the old life was at an end. They boldly demanded immediate surveys and allotments, more and better schools, cash, or cattle and tools, instead of rations and annuities, and above all, work for the young men. These were the ones who should have been heard.

The Sioux bill of 1888 offered only fifty cents an acre for much of their best land, including that along the White and Cheyenne rivers, where the two railroads proposed to push their lines through to the Black Hills. The money was not to be paid until collected from homesteaders, a provision which gave general dissatisfaction. John Grass and other leaders asserted in plain words what has since proved to be a fact—that a great deal of the land was unfit for farming and would not be taken up or, if claims were entered, they would later be abandoned. They demanded a dollar and a quarter with immediate payment in money or goods.

Notwithstanding that their trusted missionaries, or some of them, argued in favor of acceptance, I was not enthusiastic about the bill. I saw clearly, of course, that radical changes were both necessary and desirable, but I was not convinced that to part immediately with almost half their land would be to their ultimate advantage. Indeed, some of that very land is already being repurchased by the government for the use of the Sioux![1]

At the first meeting the law was explained in detail, and soon after Captain Pratt left for Washington to confer with Secretary [of the Interior William F.] Vilas. The council adjourned over Sunday and by Tuesday more than the necessary three-fourths had signed the "black paper" giving consent.[2] This they did, by their own statement, in order to secure a better title to a separate reserve, to insure continuance of schools for their children, and (by the more enlightened) to obtain individual holdings, railroad facilities, and many white neighbors. Few would have signed, however, had they not been assured that the land would be pronounced "chiefly fit for grazing purposes," which meant that each head of a family would receive three hundred and twenty acres. We are now told that from one to two square miles is necessary for the support of a family by cattle raising.

When the order came from Washington for a general council of representatives from all six of the agencies to meet immediately at Lower Brulé, the

1. During the so-called Indian New Deal of the 1930s and '40s the policy of attempting to break up reservations by allotting the lands in severalty was reversed because it had resulted in the loss by many Indians of their land and thus their means of subsistence. Since their remaining lands were inadequate to support them, the government began a land-purchase program to reconsolidate reservations and provide an adequate land base, particularly in areas unsuited to small farming.

2. "Two papers were offered in differently colored inks, and the Indians informed that every qualified voter must sign one or the other—the black paper signifying *Yes*, and the red paper, *No*. This novelty was coldly received, even met with hints that 'the red paper might turn black' by the time it reached Washington" (Elaine Goodale Eastman, *Pratt, the Red Man's Moses* [Norman: University of Oklahoma Press, 1935], p. 175).

The meeting between Pratt and Vilas actually took place in Madison, Wisconsin.

local sense of importance increased and interest was keen. Pine Ridge, Rosebud, and Cheyenne River sent influential chiefs like Swift Bird, High Bear, American Horse, and alert native policemen such as Captain Sword and Lieutenant Fast Horse. Sitting Bull at first refused to come. He later followed on horseback but made no speeches.

The "Big Council" convened in the open air on the twenty-fourth of September with an even greater crowd of absorbed spectators. Although the women had no vote then, their intelligent interest was apparent to one who heard the matter debated in family groups from end to end of the reservation. Little knots of men, some in blankets, some in natty blue uniforms or clerical black, dotted the sunburnt prairie between speeches, talking together in quiet tones as the decorated pipes of ceremony passed from hand to hand. Each delegation held a private caucus.

As usual, the official statements were patronizing in tone, addressing the Indians as if they were children incapable of reason. "Remember," Judge Wright declaimed, "it is the Great Father's hand that feeds and clothes you; his arm protects you; his voice is calling upon you to hold tight to that hand in future." In reality, no Sioux spoke of the President in such terms. Their name for him was the honorable one of "Grandfather." Their attitude was not one of awe or childlike trust—far from it!

A few speakers announced their acceptance of the offer as it stood. Among them was our own Medicine Bull, whose heart had been changed by the influence of his son Sam, educated at Hampton. It soon appeared, however, that a large majority of delegates stood with the opposition. A "secret" council of

Indians only was called for the evening in a large, empty storeroom.

I gained admission to this meeting in the character of a reporter. Sitting among them on the floor in a dense cloud of willow-scented tobacco smoke, I took notes assiduously, translating the speeches as I wrote. The same points were made, but with more freedom and picturesque emphasis. Definitely, I was on their side!

Next morning, to my surprise, Captain Pratt sent for me and looked me up and down. He was a tall, imposing man with a military fashion of speech which I thought decidedly autocratic. Too, he appeared irritated by his conspicuous want of success in carrying out his mission.

Did I (he sternly inquired) understand the Dakota tongue? I assured him that I did. What right had I to attend a secret council to which no member of the commission had access? I replied that I was there as a representative of the press. The Sioux leaders, in giving me permission, had indicated their confidence that I would report them fairly to the American public.

Captain Pratt then demanded whether I had encouraged them to reject the government's offer, adding severely that so long as I was on the payroll I was bound to support whatever policy Washington chose to adopt. I said, quite frankly, that I had taken no active part in the discussions, but had listened to their views with interest, and was not convinced that they could not do better through further negotiation. I added (not a little nettled): "I am here solely in what I believe to be the best interest of the Sioux and the fact of holding a goverment post would never stand in the way of expressing my honest opinions. If necessary, I could always resign!"

The Captain said no more, and his later record for plain speaking against official acts and policies of which he disapproved suggests that he may not have been without private sympathy for my recalcitrance.

He was the outstanding exception among Indian educators in that he vigorously opposed the whole system of racial segregation and separate schools (except as a temporary expedient) and I have always admired his stand in this.

Almost at once our visitors flatly announced that they were through and ready to go home. They would sign no paper until after their representatives had been to Washington and had arranged for such changes as the commissioners were not empowered to make. This reasonable proposition had been privately conceded by the Secretary of the Interior. Delegates were chosen forthwith and a date set for the trip at government expense. My article in *The Independent* closed with these words:

> Let us hope that the Sioux people will gain concessions as will fairly repay them for the thought they have given to this matter, and for the able and successful way in which they have conducted their deliberations. We may also hope that the measure will be accepted in the end and that it may be found, in the words of one of their number, the promise of life to future generations.

Two alert and agreeable young men fresh from college served the commission as secretaries. One of them afterward married Captain Pratt's eldest daughter. The other, who lacked nothing of Celtic wit and impulsiveness, began at once to pay me marked attention. He later admitted that a wide green sash I wore with my white frock as I sat in the women's circle halfway up the tawny slope had caught his roving eye.

I own that I was not too deeply absorbed in the business of the hour to enjoy the novelty of being once more courted in a style entirely different from the timidly respectful devotion of our Hampton boys. It was possible to become sincerely attached to these young Sioux, but only in an elder-sisterly fashion. Now comes this bold son of Erin to the wild west bank of the Missouri, and in the fortnight's interval between the two councils, while I was back at my school teaching, calls every afternoon at White River Lodge.

After all, I was only twenty-four and provided with a really adequate chaperone, in the person of an elderly aunt who took her responsibilities much to heart. "Mac" and I rode together, played a little at tennis, partook demurely of tea and his favorite chocolate cake (made by myself), and flirted harmlessly under Auntie's watchful eye for a short three weeks. We never met again, though he extracted several letters by the not uncommon device of collecting and dispatching barrels and boxes to our mission. The incident had no effect on my single-minded devotion to the cause of my adopted people.

PAGAN INTERLUDE

TOWARD THE CLOSE OF MY THIRD YEAR AT White River I began to be restless. The community center was moving smoothly, quite according to plan. I was no longer pioneering. At this point, Bishop Hare offered me a remote mission outpost among the wilder Teton Sioux, an invitation not without a strong appeal. The suggestion came from an influential quarter that I might, if I wished, be promoted to the superintendency of one of the smaller government boarding schools. But the neglected, the despised day school was still my first thought. I longed for the opportunity to build up many more little camp schools, close to the lives of the people. I told myself that I would resign and go back East . . . go to Mohonk . . . to Washington! I would put the whole case before people with influence and see what could be done.

In the meantime, why not employ the long summer vacation in still further consolidating my influence with the "wilder" element? After all, up to this time my official position had set a certain distance between us, even on camping trips. I decided that nothing could be better for the purpose than an old-time deer hunt.

Whirling Hawk, an unreconstructed old pagan from the other side of White River, was planning to hunt for several weeks in the sand hills of Nebraska, the nearest point where large game might be found. I knew his two wives slightly. They were sisters as was customary when a man took more than one wife. I approached them as soon as school was out, and had no little difficulty in persuading them to carry my tent and baggage and to allow me to ride alongside on my pacing pony. They explained over and over that they might be gone a long time, and that I shouldn't like it at all—that I didn't know, in short, what I was letting myself in for. However, I persisted, paid cash in advance for the coveted privilege, and bought a supply of provisions which I turned over to the elder Mrs. Whirling Hawk. I took my meals with the family and shared alike with them throughout the journey.

The other four men of the party were middle-aged conservatives. All but one wore long hair and Indian dress; none spoke any English; and one was a well-known medicine man—always the spearhead of opposition to the "new way." Two of the younger women usually rode with me; the others, with their children and household gear, filled five covered wagons. The cavalcade was followed by several loose colts and a rabble of noisy dogs. Sioux women ride astride, but I clung to the Victorian side-saddle, even in the wilderness.

My outfit had already crossed the river and been stowed in the cabin of my respective host when his young wife, Esther, came for me on a morning of pouring rain. She was a pert, upstanding girl of about eighteen—he probably a man in his fifties. Characteristically paying no attention to the weather, they brought up my pony and helped me ford the rapidly rising stream, themselves wading waist-deep in the milky flood. We partially dried ourselves at the kitchen stove and lunched enjoyably on hot baked potatoes and baked pumpkin. There was no thought of postponing the start. "We set off about mid-afternoon" (so runs my penciled diary),

> over roads which are simply shocking, and camp a few miles out at *Chanshoka*—Thick Woods creek. In the course of half an hour, we are cozily ensconced on dry blankets, spread upon pine boughs to keep out some of the wet, before a bright fire in the middle of the tipi, talking and laughing over a good supper of toasted jerked beef, bacon, hot biscuit, potatoes, eggs, and coffee. The women of our party exchange ceremonious visits, all bringing presents of food. One gives some onions, another wild cherries. I return these favors with coffee and sugar, which are coveted luxuries. Presently we all go to sleep, and with a good fire and plenty of blankets I pass a very comfortable night.

It remained for the next day to discover that we had with us one woman shortly expecting a baby and an old man so feeble that he more than half expected to die on the road. Apparently, no one thought it strange or unsuitable that these two should embark on a rough and laborious journey! Nor was this all. One Crooked Foot and his elder wife—who turned out to be a trouble-maker—indulged in a furious quarrel and it took our united efforts to prevail upon the angry woman not to set off at once, on foot, for the home of relatives a hundred miles away.

After my first full day on horseback I was stiff and very sleepy and, in fact, fell asleep before supper was ready. I ate and slept again. Later in the night there arose a cry: "Someone comes!" Immediately all bestir themselves; the coals are raked together; the coffee pot set back on the fire; and the solitary traveler on his way back from Rosebud is welcomed with supper and a smoke.

Chasing Crane, as he is called, is full of a strange story of the second coming of Christ.

"God," he declares, "has appeared to the Crows across the Stony Mountains. They say he arrived out of nowhere, announcing himself as the Savior who once before came upon earth and was killed by the white people. He told the Indians he could no longer bear to hear parents crying for their children, dying everywhere of hunger and strange diseases brought by white men. He promised to let down the sky upon all the whites and to bring back the buffalo for our use. The Messiah was beautiful to look upon, with waving hair. He bore paint as a sign of power."

All listened spellbound as to a revelation from heaven to these words out of the night and the vast empty spaces. Presently the men prepared a vapor bath (which had for them a religious as well as a hygienic meaning), and I fell asleep once more to the soothing, monotonous beat of ritual songs—never dreaming of the strange and cruel events destined to grow out of Chasing Crane's fantastic story.

The next night brought a violent thunderstorm with a gale of wind. Although everything had been made as snug as possible—tent pins driven in firmly and poles well braced—the tipi seemed about to collapse upon our heads. We all sat up. The women silently stirred the fire and the old man smoked steadily—perhaps as a sacrifice to the spirits, perhaps merely to keep his courage up. Indians are fearful and superstitious about many things, among them the "thunder-bird" with fiery beak. I recall another furious storm on the prairies where a number of us were camping together. Suddenly the night was filled with the wailing that means death. A woman in a nearby tent had been instantly killed with zig-zag burns, they told me, down all one side from shoulder to heel.

By the fourth or fifth day of wilderness travel, we began to pass an occasional sod shanty with stable of the same, a stack of wild hay, and a few rods of wire fencing—the rustic homestead of some pioneer Nebraskan. Gaunt women, in ugly calico frocks and sunbonnets, came to their doors to stare at us with natural curiosity. Making camp at night near a small settlement, we were hardly up in time next morning to meet the visitors, all eager to see what they could, to ask questions, to try to "make a trade."

Our people had little to offer except some beadwork and a few superfluous garments from the last issue. The sand-hillers persistently tried to tempt them with offers of broken-down hacks and worthless old shotguns. Horse racing was the favorite sport of both parties. Neither had any cash to speak of and efforts to communicate by signs were sufficiently funny. I was constantly pressed into service as interpreter, but reserved the right to decline when I disapproved of the business in hand.

There was a small store in the place and the men sold the moccasins off their feet in their eagerness to buy ammunition, rope, tobacco, and coffee. There was some difficulty about the first, possibly a local law against sale to Indians. Ranchmen brought us chickens, eggs, and green corn, and we made a delicious meal. The men were urged to give a dance but Nebraskans couldn't raise enough money to tempt them.

A wistful-eyed young man from a forlorn "soddy" lingered near our tipi after the others had gone, indulging in long confidences about himself, his family back home, and his growing herd. A bachelor of twenty-seven, he lamented his lonely life on the claim and wound up by asking, shyly enough, if I would be willing to correspond with him. I had been assured everywhere, no doubt with truth, that "it's hard for a girl to stay single in this country." Love laughs at dictionaries, and my two "sisters," sitting close by, were openly amused by what they interpreted as a budding romance. I was relieved to know that my bashful caller, evidently on his good behavior, could not translate their too frank comments. Though I've forgotten his name, I dare say he is long since a solid citizen—perhaps a cattle king!

The courage of these pioneers, most of them used to comparative comfort "back east"—by which they usually meant Iowa or Illinois—might have had a stronger appeal for me had I not been already identified with the cause of the dispossessed red man. I thought a "soddy" far less attractive than a log cabin. They were built of bricks about three feet long, cut from the virgin sod, the best ones roofed and floored with rough boards, a few even lined with cotton cloth. I was told that a man alone could put up one of the primitive kind in a week.

The Sioux were on the whole living better at the time and showed some contempt for the white man's poverty. Corn and cattle seemed to be the main dependence, though here and there were gardens filled with tempting vegetables. Some women confessed that they had lived for weeks on literally nothing but cornbread and gravy, or perhaps mush and milk. I saw lace curtains, framed photographs, and a copy of Moore's *Poems*[1] in a wretched one-room hut, occupied by several barefoot children and a hollow-eyed little mother, refined in speech and manner, though shoeless and in rags.

At a large hay camp, the sturdy young sister of the ranchman seemed well content. She spent the nights, or some of them, on her own claim close by, and the days herding her brother's cattle and helping him make hay. They invited me to dine with them on green corn and boiled pumpkins. After which I rode with the girl to her shack and we drove home the cows. My diary comments: "They live in a wretched shanty, but are nice people."

At every stream or pond we bathed and washed our clothes—with soap, if we had it. The loose Dakota dress permits of dressing and undressing in the open without exposure, since a dry frock is simply put over the wet one on coming out of the water, and the latter slipped off underneath. I found the Dakotas far more cleanly under primitive conditions than are most of us habitual house-dwellers when camping out. I lived and slept within a few feet of them for weeks at a time, yet never saw a Sioux woman take off all her clothes or indeed expose any part of her body. While nursing her baby, the breast was completely concealed by the wide sleeve. This Dakota dress—which I myself wore much of the time on the trip—is, I believe, the most modest ever devised. The men were more scantily clad—occasionally in no more than is considered proper on a modern bathing beach—but they, too, were decently covered at all times.

Nearing the Niobrara River, called "Running Water" by the Sioux, we reached a seemingly impassable

---

1. No doubt the Irish poet Thomas Moore, popular at the time, whose lyrics included "Believe Me if All Those Endearing Young Charms" and "The Harp That Once through Tara's Halls."

canyon, bristling with pines. The men literally carved a rough road around rocks and stumps, and the loaded wagons descended slowly but in safety. Women and children eagerly gathered spruce gum and wild cherries, or hunted for *teepsinna*, a fibrous root with a sweetish taste, described by an early explorer as "halfway between a turnip and a mushroom." It may be eaten raw or boiled with meat. The men found some red willow and stripped the aromatic bark, which is dried and mixed with tobacco for a satisfying smoke.

We found a courageous widow living in a log hut right on the river bank, with her large family of little ones. We made friends at once and I baked a large batch of biscuit in her oven while Whirling Hawk bargained for one of her litter of piglings, which was quickly dressed and roasted whole for an excellent supper. My diary constantly stresses this matter of food, always of first importance when one gets down to the bare essentials of living. I know it was constantly in our thoughts, whether consisting of wild game as new to me as badger, skunk, and mud turtle, or mere bread and coffee—even when the coffee had run out, of tea made from wild mint or rose-hips or the leaves of some bush known to the Indians. Meat was scarce and we had not as yet seen any deer.

Pressing steadily on through a land of sunshine, sand, and sunflowers, the crests of the low hills appeared white as snow, while elsewhere the ground was sparsely clothed with thin grass. There were no trees, nor even bushes, except the sand cherry, a low shrub covered with astringent black fruit the size of a small plum. The Sioux had an odd saying that it was eatable only if approached against the wind. The dead roots and branches, together with cow chips, provided our only fuel, making it necessary to cook over a very small fire. Between the Loup and the

Platte, the Dismal and the Big Blue rivers, we found no water except small lakes strongly impregnated with alkali, and the occasional wells at ranches and railway stations.[2] Not only was the alkali water unfit to drink by man or beast, but when I once ventured on a bath in such a pond the color all came out of my bright blue frock and my skin burned for hours after.

One day, as we crawled languidly over the unmarked prairie in the July heat, I was startled to see men and boys leap suddenly from their seats and race ahead of the wagons, yelling and throwing off their clothes as they ran. Surely, I thought, there could be no enemy in sight! Soon, all were dashing into a shallow pond, madly chasing a flock of half-grown wild ducks, not yet able to fly. Screaming with joy, they plunged after the terrified birds as they dove and rose and dove again, finally seizing and wringing their necks and casting them triumphantly on shore. Several women and girls followed the men into the water, while for my own part I sat on the muddy bank and laughed until I could laugh no more. It was all so gay and so perfectly spontaneous, even to plucking the ducks (saving the down for pillows), and putting them at once over the fire for an impromptu feast.

---

2. The reference here to the Big Blue River (which is in southeastern Nebraska, well away from the route traveled) must be a slip of the pen for Blue Creek, at the western edge of the sand hills.

BIRTH AND DEATH ON THE PRAIRIE

THE WOMEN NOW TOOK THEIR TURNS AT DRIV-
ing the teams, while the five men scoured the hills on
horseback, impatiently looking for game. "The long-
expected event" (I wrote one night in my diary),

> Whirling Thunder brings home booty—a female antelope—
> the skin and pretty head hanging from one side of the saddle,
> the meat from the other. He is handed a cup of coffee and his
> pipe, and gravely offers thanks to the spirits before smoking.
> His wives divide the venison among the five families, eagerly
> devouring the raw liver and tripe. In ten minutes, I have
> lightly broiled and am eating my portion of the former, and a
> great pot of venison is on the fire. We are meat-hungry, and it
> tastes good! Presently, the unsuccessful hunters appear and
> are invited to supper. Hot broth and coffee, great dishes of
> smoking meat, filled pipes, and long reminiscences of other
> days fill a merry evening around the fire in the big tent.

It was the invariable custom to share the fruits of
the chase equally, or nearly so, and whatever provision might be bought or begged on the way usually
met the same fate. All fared alike—the lucky and the

unlucky, the energetic and the lazy—though not, as will appear later, without some complaints. When plenty reigned we all feasted, and in times of scarcity we fasted together, nor would any other arrangement have been possible under those conditions. Constant activity in the open air and a few days of short commons so sharpened our appetites that the savory smell of a haunch of tender venison, turning slowly on a stick over a fine bed of coals, was an almost unendurable temptation. Once I was left to watch such a roast alone when some mysterious alarm was given and all the others vanished suddenly for what seemed a long time. It was long enough, they always declared, for the dinner to be half gone when they came back. Indians dearly love to "rag," and we never met again in after years but that I was joyously reminded of this more or less fictitious incident.

The women's labors were many and cheerfully performed. I have never seen them treated as "slaves" or "beasts of burden," but always as equals and companions. They laughed and chatted freely with husbands and near relatives—especially brothers-in-law, with whom a certain jesting familiarity was permitted—advised and scolded them much as women do their menfolk all over the world. It was certainly no hardship for them to fetch the wood and water, take down and put up the tipi, or even water and harness the ponies upon occasion—though this task was commonly assigned to the bigger boys. When the ordinary work of the camp was done, my Dakota "sisters" set about gathering, pounding, and drying wild cherries, picked mint and balm, scraped and tanned skins, and made or mended moccasins. I never cared to handle a gun, but took care of my own pony and shared in the women's work except for dressing meat and tanning skins. Their method took but a short time and left the skin beautifully soft and white. If they wanted to give it the deep yellow tint that is more useful for hard wear, they smoked it over a pit filled with burning sagebrush. Moccasins sold freely to the settlers at a dollar a pair.

Rattlesnakes were common and before going into camp near a prairie dog town, where they abounded, it was customary to beat the ground thoroughly. I saw many killed and was sometimes presented with the rattles.

I think it was on the Loup that a charming little waterfall, called "Whispering Water" by the Sioux, sang so loud that my pony refused to go near. I dismounted and went to admire it while the others made camp. Soon Whirling Hawk signaled with his blanket for his fastest pony. Esther went to his aid and they had a hard chase after a wounded buck, bringing him in after dark in the teeth of a violent thunder shower. One windy morning, my cotton dress caught from the campfire and was extinguished just in time by one of the women. Such were some of the unforeseen excitements that varied our days.

Though in those years the settlers were a hard-riding, rough-spoken set, to say the least—and traditionally there was "no law west of the Missouri River"—my own experience was uniformly pleasant. At a large cattle ranch with extensive buildings, we found ten young American cowboys and a more mannerly, good-humored crowd one could hardly hope to meet anywhere. They called upon us in a body after the day's work was done, and the great herd of seven hundred longhorns massed on the shores of a large alkali lake gave forth a sound like distant thunder.

One gentlemanly youth was anxious to buy a pair of moccasins. "But fifty-five cents is all I have in the world," he naively declared, pulling a handful of silver out of his breeches pocket and looking at it with a comical air of concern. "Can't you make it up for me, fellows?"

One handed over a quarter, another a dime. "Thank you! Only ten cents more!" Somebody dug up three copper cents. It finally appeared that ninety-three cents was all they could get together among them, and this the owner of the moccasins was persuaded to accept.

"Why, if that isn't my brand on them!" the young man exclaimed, scanning the beaded pattern with delight. "Evidently they were always meant for me!'"

"Do any of you shoot wolves?" another inquired. "The boss will pay five dollars apiece for their scalps. They kill no end of calves." We heard later of bounties up to twenty-five dollars being offered by cattlemen, but none was earned by our party. I think traps and poison were more successful methods for ridding the range of this pest.

Settlers everywhere we went were friendly and even generous to the Indians, showing no trace of ill-feeling. One day Whirling Hawk—familiarly called "Limpy" in Sioux, though the slight lameness resulting from an old knife wound never kept him quiet—came home proudly displaying the third hat that had been given him since we started, none of which he ever thought of wearing. Someone gave him an old pair of trousers and these his wife cut over into leggings, worn with a gay calico shirt and a cotton bandanna wound turban-wise about grizzled locks. It entertained him vastly to pose as a destitute wanderer and invite gifts of all kinds, merely in order to make endless fun of gift and giver. He begged regularly for unneeded food, on the theory that he was collecting a debt from the greedy white man on the instalment plan, and had no hesitation at all, after enjoying two hearty breakfasts at his own and a-other's fireside, in asserting that he hadn't tasted a mouthful for two days. Really, the old fellow was a humorist!

"A strange, uncouth landscape," comments my diary. "Today we rode into the queerest little town—half a dozen board and sod shanties, smothered in immense sunflowers and clouds of sand." The town was called Whitman and had the great advantage of a location on the railroad. Besides the station and freight house, it contained two stores, a "saloon and restaurant," and the office of the county clerk. I was told that actual residents numbered just fifteen, but that many land-seekers and hunters traded there.

I made the acquaintance of the saloonkeeper's wife—once more "a nice little woman—lives in a queer, bare place"—was invited to supper and re-ported the supper good. I arranged to have my mail forwarded there and rode over ten days later on the noon freight from Bingham, then merely a section-house where trains would stop on signal. On this second visit I collected twelve overdue letters—one with a welcome check from a magazine—was kindly entertained overnight and slept little, what with a poor bed, hosts of fleas, and racket of trains at midnight when the passenger train went through. This was my only night indoors in nine long weeks. Being again in funds, I bought some fruit and candy wherewith to treat my fellow-campers, and came back next day on the freight, sitting gaily up aloft, sharing a watermelon with the genial conductor.

It gave me no little amusement throughout the trip to be accosted by strangers—plainly meaning no offense—with: "Can you talk American?," "Why, you've been to school, I guess!," or (doubtfully) "Were both your parents white folks?" True, I wore a calico frock and moccasins, with my sun-bleached hair in a long braid down my back, donning shoes and a hat only when going to town, and a naturally clear skin was deeply tanned from constant exposure. In spite of appearances, no one was less than civil and it would have been the simplest thing possible to stop off somewhere and "grow up with the country."

In one ambitious hamlet, I was not only asked to Sunday school and Sunday dinner with one of the leading citizens (an invitation promptly accepted), but after further conversation was warmly pressed to take charge of the just built district school, of which they were intensely proud. Even if, in a moment of discouragement, a half-starved homesteader might assert the sand hills to be "the very worst country on the face of God's green earth," I was likely to read next day in some smudged local sheet the truly American boast: "Come to the Arcadia and El Dorado, the Elysium and Hesperides of the world!" (This is a literal quotation.)

Among our callers from time to time were typical parties of emigrants in well-filled covered wagons, parties of big-game hunters returning from the Bighorn Mountains, and a "chicken outfit" tenting nearby—pot-hunters killing prairie chickens in quantity for city markets. A nice old man, who said he had taught school forty-two terms, showed us the rain gauge and thermometers with which he took official observations for the Weather Bureau, as well as a map on which for the first time I traced our route, covering some four hundred miles.

Yellow Eyes, our medicine man, treated the schoolteacher's son and daughter by request, actually receiving one dollar for professional services! Others met were the county commissioner, who telegraphed an item about us to the Omaha paper, and the county superintendent of schools with his pretty, soft-spoken wife. She inquired mildly whether I traveled with Indians "to keep them in order." One man suggested that I take them east as a "show." "There's dollars in it!" (And so it has proved, both then and since, but showmanship was never in my line.) A traveling photographer insisted upon taking a group photograph—the men standing at attention, gun in hand, while we women, heavily shawled, sat meekly in a row in the middle foreground.

The only dull days were the occasional rainy ones, when there wasn't a thing to do but sit in the tent on a pile of damp quilts and listen to the same inter-minable tales, told over and over again. I used to work rather half-heartedly on a pair of moccasins that I was awkwardly trying to embroider with stiff porcupine quills, and long for something—any-thing—to read. (I had brought no book except a pocket Testament in Dakota.) There were days, too, when a meat diet would pall and the craving for fresh fruits and something sweet would become a torment. Once a stolen handful of green apples set me to baking a "pie" in a frying pan.

I have been asked whether the plain speech of the Sioux was not offensive, and would answer that the women's chatter was like that of a child—too matter-of-fact to be obscene. Since there are no polite circumlocutions in the language, they, of course, called a spade a spade. Profanity in Sioux is un-known. Perhaps from instinctive delicacy, the men were careful of their speech in my presence. The superstitious dread of taking food from the hand of a woman undergoing her "mysterious" monthly ordeal was still current, and I had been warned that it might lead to embarrassing questions. However, I was spared any personal reference to *isnati*—the solitary lodge.

Antelope were now abundant. Once a herd of thirty was seen, of whom six fell to the hunter—a time of plenty and rejoicing! Whirling Hawk was by far the best marksman in the party and his elder wife, a motherly, good-humored creature, shared freely with the other four families. However, jealousy and ill-feeling developed between her and Mrs. Blackstone, a notoriously bad-tempered woman, ending in a general war of words and even worse. One day when I happened to be away from camp, my hostess was not only vehemently accused of stinginess—the unforgivable sin—but actually attacked with a hatchet! The two women were separated by the men before any damage was done, and the Blackstones naturally packed up and departed immediately.

A few days later, a little girl was born to Mrs. Crooked Foot the younger on the open prairie. There were a few minutes of confusion and much running to and fro, with calls for a sharp knife and a piece of string. Soon the baby was carried home by a friend, neatly done up in an oblong bundle, and the mother walked unaided to her place in the tent. The incident caused less excitement than the discovery of a beaver dam at about the same time, and far less than the quarrel I have described.

While we were still some two hundred miles from White River, returning unhurriedly by a different route, our unconventional journey ended suddenly in stark tragedy. As everyone knows, it was and still is illegal to sell liquor to Indians (except citizens off the reservation). Now and then, the men contrived to buy a bottle of "painkiller" or lemon extract and indulged in a mild spree. So I thought nothing of it when partly aroused one night by distant sounds of revelry.

Next morning, Whirling Hawk did not stir. His young wife bent over him, found him stiff and cold, and started back with a shriek. Instantly, screams rent the air and the camp was thrown into confusion as the death became known.

My questions brought information that Yellow Eyes had secured something to drink—no one knew what—at a solitary store a few miles behind us, that all had partaken of it and had suffered with chills and severe nausea. Fortunately, all but one recovered. I made them drive me back. The terrified store-keeper, when I told him what had happened, swore that the Indian had only a bottle of harmless "bitters" together with a tincture of aconite in another bottle. He had pretended this last was for a sick horse. It seemed that they had combined the two, and that only the quantity of the poison, producing active vomiting, had saved the lives of the others.

The man was badly frightened, and made no difficulty when ordered to provide a coffin. The body was placed in the rough pine box, lifted into the wagon, and we set out for home, breakfastless and miserable. The two widows cried and wailed aloud until so hoarse that they could no longer utter a sound. It was now late in September and the weather began to be cold. It was after dark when we made camp. The women instantly set to work on a new shirt for the dead man. They refused to eat. I was given a little hot food—the first that day—in Crooked Foot's tent and went to bed worn out.

Without a taste of hardship as well as pleasure, my experience of primitive life would not have been the real thing. Of course, I might have made for the nearest way-station on my pony and taken the train for Chamberlain. Unthinkable to abandon my two "sisters" in their bitter distress! According to custom, they had immediately given away their whole stock of food and their pots and pans. Provision for the three devolved entirely upon me. They would not cook and were hardly to be prevailed upon to eat what I prepared. This record of the second day after the catastrophe is taken from my diary:

> Up before sunrise—no food until late afternoon—got into camp after dark in a steady rain, without a scrap of anything to burn. Esther and I take the ponies to water, and call at a house half a mile away to beg a little wood. We get it, dry ourselves by the fire, and go to bed. Forty miles today.

It had been, I suspect, in the back of my mind to meet that persuasive, blue-eyed bachelor once more, but the fates ruled otherwise. "A kind ranchman helped us up a bad hill," I wrote, "but it was not *the* one." We crossed the Niobrara in safety, first staking out the ford and putting four horses to each wagon. Then, says the record, "we three women hurry on ahead of the others and travel at top speed until too dark to see. I buy a loaf of rye bread at a settler's cabin and we make a dry camp."

By this time, the overworked horses are ready to give out. Even my own petted gray must be whipped and urged continually, taking his turn in harness, while from the back of the wagon the sad, cold odor of mortality is already diffused upon the air.

We reach home on the fifth day and send for Mr. Walker to conduct a funeral service over our pagan leader. I recall our tolerant minister's generous praise of the widows, who had done their duty as they saw it, in bringing their dead to lie among his kindred on the bluffs above the tawny river. It was a strange ceremony. Mrs. Whirling Hawk's bare legs are criss-crossed with bleeding red lines. Her hair is chopped off short; the fringes are gone from her ragged shawl; and in the pauses of the prayer book ritual all the women wail aloud, as if mourning a world that is lost.

BREAKING NEW TRAILS

WHEN I WENT EAST AGAIN IN THE AUTUMN OF
1889, I had no money and no job, but I had ideas to
spare and plenty of self-confidence. Believing that I
knew the Sioux and their needs, I had made definite
plans for my next campaign. Looking back upon a
long and disillusioning experience, I am amazed by
such rashness on the part of a young woman barely
twenty-six years old without family or political back-
ing and lacking even a college diploma! I knew,
however, that I possessed the confidence of two
authorities on the Indian, General Armstrong and
Bishop Hare, each of whom gave me a letter to the
Commissioner of Indian Affairs. The Bishop wrote:

> Miss Elaine Goodale's deep and intelligent interest in the
> Indians, her high purpose, skill as an educator, and familiar-
> ity with the Indians in their daily life in their homes, would
> make her, in my opinion, a valuable auxiliary to your depart-
> ment.

General Armstrong's letter ran in part:

This will introduce Miss Elaine Goodale, for three years a teacher at White River Camp, Dakota, where she built up the model day school for the reservation. She has studied and been into Indian life as have few in this country. I think it would be fortunate for the Indian Department to secure her services.

As it happened, these generous introductions were never used or needed and I still possess the originals.

Mother had moved to the city of Northampton, Massachusetts, the better to educate the three younger children, two of whom attended Smith College. She allowed me to make her modest home my headquarters while I embarked upon a series of paid talks and newspaper articles upon my chosen theme. I spoke straight from the heart, without timidity or formal preparation, in New York, Philadelphia, Hartford, Worcester, and other cities. Several meetings were arranged by Mr. Herbert Welsh of the Indian Rights Association, my escort on that first visit to Dakota; others by Mrs. A. S. Quinton, first president of the Women's National Indian Association. I was presently invited to address churches and schools, and even a Grange. For the first time, it seemed desirable to own a "platform frock" of handsome brocaded silk in my favorite shades of brown.

All this, of course, was only preliminary to my real purpose, and I should probably not have gotten far but for the happy coincidence that this precise moment placed a trained educator at the head of Indian affairs. It is a chair usually occupied, then and since, by a routine politician. I did not have to seek out General Thomas J. Morgan, the Indian Commissioner just selected by President Harrison. We spoke from the same platform and sometimes traveled together from one engagement to the next. I discovered to my joy that General Morgan had clear-cut plans for the reform and organization of a hitherto disorderly and inefficient Indian school system. He saw in me a ready instrument toward their realization. When he asked me for my program for community day schools and gave it full approval, it seemed that the first battle was won! Witness an extract from a paper published in Worcester, Massachusetts, in the month of November 1889:

Miss Elaine Goodale, a pretty Yankee girl well known to lovers of good literature, who has been a teacher at the Hampton Indian school and later engaged in work among the Dakotas, was introduced (to a lecture audience in the city) and told a very interesting story of her work in establishing a day school in one of the wild tribes. At the close General Morgan said he would tell a secret. Upon his return to Washington, he intended to appoint Miss Goodale the supervisor of the day school system in the Dakotas, provided he had the means at his command, and the appointment can undoubtedly be considered as made.

It was not quite so simple as this, however. General Morgan's own appointment had not yet been confirmed by the Senate, owing to active opposition from the Roman Catholic church, which held contracts for educating Indian children in a number of ecclesiastically manned boarding schools. Morgan had made no secret of the fact that he was not in favor of subsidizing any religious body with federal funds. He demanded immediate public provision for all Indian children, except those of the Five Civilized Tribes, who had developed schools of their own, and those enrolled in missionary institutions of high standing. The new commissioner called for a complete graded school system with trained teachers and effective supervision. He would ask Congress for three and a half million dollars to begin with and "Congress will give it, if the people say so."

It was not until several years later that civil service rules were extended to the Indian Service. Morgan had been asked to appoint old soldiers unfit for active work, old schoolmasters broken in health, small politicians who had helped in the last election. He had been urged to put an incompetent at the head of an important school "in order to save Ohio." He, on the other hand, in addition to training and experience, was looking, as he said, for "youth, health, and enthusiasm."

I, too, had been campaigning for teachers of the right type. After speaking at one normal school, nine of the young women gave me their names as candidates for the Indian Service upon graduation.

While waiting, I naturally supported General Morgan's program and urged his confirmation in the pages of *The Independent, Evangelist, Arena, Lend-a-Hand*, and other journals of the day. Morgan's special fitness was so well known that he had been offered a choice between the commissionerships of Education and Indian Affairs. After some delay, during which he continued to act, the Senate confirmed the appointment. Soon afterward, I went down to Washington to claim in person the fulfillment of his promise to me, made almost on our first interview.

I had expected merely to be placed in charge of day schools among the Sioux, but the Commissioner prevailed upon the President and Secretary of the Interior [John W.] Noble to create a new office—that of Supervisor of Education in the two Dakotas—and I became the first incumbent. Several large boarding schools were included in this district.

Since it was now up to me to blaze new trails, I had thought out the technique of such an office very carefully, basing it partly on Bishop Hare's method

of covering the same field in the absence of inns and
all public carriers. I had many long talks with Pro-
fessor [Charles C.] Painter, then the Washington
representative of the Indian Rights Association, who
with Mrs. Painter earned my gratitude by many little
acts of kindness, as well as much good advice. It had
been customary to allow traveling expenses for field
work. I boldly demanded a team of horses, wagon,
and complete camping outfit with a Sioux couple of
my own choice as driver and cook. Thus, I might be
sure of protection and chaperonage at all times. The
matter of salary was, with me, a secondary consid-
eration and I was content to be allotted a very small
one for so responsible a post—one which was, in fact,
increased by fifty percent for the benefit of my male
successor and has since been more than doubled.

Believing that day schools could be made efficient
for elementary training at less than half the cost of
boarding schools and with little or no opposition
from parents, I urged that they be better equipped to
help adult Indians as well as children. At Mohonk,
my resolution to that effect was made a part of the
platform of the conference. I presented tentative
plans for an improved school building with teacher's
residence attached, estimated to cost double the
six-hundred-dollar limit then in vogue. In those days
of extremely modest appropriations, the notion of a
thirty-thousand-dollar day school building could
have occurred to no one in his senses, still less the use
of school buses to collect Indian children from their
homes! It was necessary that they live within walking
distance.

It developed that I must pay my own salary and
that of my two assistants, as well as assume financial
responsibility for all personal equipment, and for this
purpose I was made a "special disbursing officer" and
instructed in the preparation of elaborate sworn

accounts by a clerk in the Indian Office. Next I was handed a short letter to all Indian agents. Thus armed, I went back to my aunt at White River Lodge, there engaged as helpers a Hampton-educated couple whom I knew well, bought a team and outfit in Chamberlain, covered the Brulé and Crow Creek schools, and set out in May for the western agencies.

A few weeks later, a special dispatch from Washington appeared in the *New York Evening Post*. It ran in part as follows:

> Miss Elaine Goodale's work among the Sioux Indians of the two Dakotas in the exercise of her office as supervisor of education is attracting much attention at the Indian Bureau, her communications from the field being wonderfully business-like, candid, and specific in detail. Commissioner Morgan has supplied her with a wagon and camping outfit, as there are no railroads or regular stage conveyances in the country through which her labors carry her, and has hired an Indian man to drive and his wife to do the cooking for the party. This makes her entirely independent, and she is busily engaged in inspecting and reporting upon the condition of the schools.
>
> Her territory is large, embracing a greater number of these institutions than any other state or territory. . . . Of sixty schools, forty-nine are wholly supported by the goverment, nine by religious societies under contracts by which the government pays annual sums ranging from $108 to $175 per annum for the care of each pupil and his tuition, and two by the government and a religious society combined.
>
> Considerable criticism was provoked by the choice of a young, unmarried woman for the work in this wild Dakota country, but the Commissioner reasoned that . . . one who had already proved her mettle as Miss Goodale has, and whose training was so thorough in all directions, would make a more striking impression upon the Indians than a man. He is very desirous, now that the Sioux—an especially strong and vigorous nation—are coming gradually out of the tribal relation and into recognition of the rights and responsibilities of the individual, to turn their thoughts as much as possible toward education, as the key to the problems that confront them in their new estate.

Such freedom and power of initiative as I now possessed was thoroughly congenial and I never complained of the lack of specific instructions. I was responsible directly to the Commissioner, who invited me to write him confidentially whenever I wished, in addition to my official communications, which were illustrated by my own camera—a custom less common than it is today. He encouraged, and indeed desired, me to continue writing for the press with my accustomed frankness, and I took full advantage of his permission to take the public into our confidence.

Upon one occasion, and only one, this habit made a little trouble for us both. A published criticism of a contract school came to the attention of the Catholic Indian Bureau and was made the subject of formal protest at Washington. The Commissioner felt compelled to send me an official reprimand, but the sting was almost removed by the receipt, in the same mail, of a personal letter in which he exonerated me of any real indiscretion. General Armstrong wrote me about this same article in *The Independent*: "It is excellent— wise and fair. You have found just fault with Catholic schools and some of their teachers admit that you are right. Your point about inquiring into and inspecting contract schools is sound, and you can greatly improve them while securing their respect by being candid."

After much acrimonious debate, this system was abolished by Congress and ended in 1901. However, certain tribal and trust funds are still used for the purpose when petition is made by the tribe in question.

A YEAR ON WHEELS

THE "BIG CATS," AS THE SIOUX CALLED ALL
government inspectors, were really not too subtle in
their tactics. They were almost always personal guests
of the Indian agent, their coming heralded well in
advance from end to end of the reservation, and
hasty preparations made accordingly. Relieved of the
embarrassment of forcing the hospitality of strangers, particularly those with whom I had official rela-
tions, I took care to arrive unannounced, taking in
the outlying camps first of all. A teacher's first intima-
tion of my existence, on this initial round, was often
my appearance at the schoolhouse door. I would
introduce myself briefly, decline the offer of a seat on
the platform, slip into one near the door where my
presence would disturb the children as little as possible, and request that the exercises proceed exactly
as usual.

If we arrived after school hours at the little L-
shaped building with belfry atop (usually in a creek
bottom, tree-fringed and in the middle of a strag-

gling settlement of tipis and log cabins), we would
first make camp in a convenient grove. When the
teacher came out to investigate, he might find me
seated cozily on an improvised divan under an awning, writing up the day's notes in longhand, or
possibly out by the creek with rod and line, trying to
catch a few fish for supper.

Girls in those days didn't wear breeches, slacks, or
shorts, and I thought to strike a happy medium
between comfort and convention by adopting a simple one-piece dress, made in gingham or flannel
according to the weather, and worn with a soft hat
and moccasins. The mountain wagon provided for
my use was roomy and substantial. Tent, mess-chest,
and canvas-covered rolls of bedding for the three of
us were strapped on behind. Buckets, coffee pot, and
lantern dangled at the sides, while valises, camera,
gun, and miscellaneous impedimenta filled every
available inch of space beneath and around the
occupants. A good team of blacks hauled us over
unmarked and often difficult trails. The wheels drag
heavily in the sand. On the down grades, the driver
jams on the brakes and the big horses hold back with
all their might. At the bottom, there is a steep gully or
one of the little creeks that intersect this vast empty
landscape with a network of tributary streams, all
flowing into the White River.

The shotgun, by the way, was carried for the sole
purpose of adding occasional small game to our usual
fare of canned goods, bacon, biscuit, and coffee.
While Leon is stealing up on a flock of plover, trying
to get two of the birds in line, an old Indian on a
small white pony overtakes the wagon.

The schoolhouse, he says, is just at the foot of the
next hill. Has he a child in school? He has. Is it a good
school? Yes, they have a good teacher. There is only

one thing that doesn't please him. Many of the children walk a long way to school, stay until the sun is low, and walk home again, and all that time they eat nothing but one hardtack and part of a cup of coffee.

Scant attention had thus far been paid to the views of patrons, but ability to speak Dakota fluently and correctly proved an instant passport to their confidence. I consulted them freely and often found my reasoned conclusions anticipated by these intuitive and keen judges of human nature. They resented an indifferent or patronizing attitude and despised a grafter. In this case, there is no doubt that the little ones were ill fed and had been known to faint in class from hunger.

There was implied compliment to the Sioux in the very fact of my choosing to speak their tongue although it was not required of me, in my frank enjoyment of their company, my habitual wearing of moccasins, and my choice of the Dakota lodge over every other form of canvas house. Its merits, indeed, were admitted when it was made the model for the Sibley army tent. It is roomier and prettier than a wall tent, less liable to overturn in a high wind, and is ventilated as well as warmed by the central fire with opening above. The chimney flaps, properly regulated, carry off most of the smoke and the whole is easily transformed in a few minutes into a breezy awning for summer weather.

Although the native policeman, looking dignified and responsible in natty blue uniform, might often be found beside the door as a symbol, it was rarely necessary to compel, or even to urge, attendance at day schools. The Indian's need of the white man's tools was obvious enough. He might be inclined to allow but two or three years at most for an education, but that misconception was bound to disappear in time. I was sometimes taken out behind an Indian team to view the location they had agreed upon among themselves for another little school, and to verify their count of the required thirty children within walking distance.

Even the natural objections to distant boarding schools could be largely overcome with patience and discretion. I advised them only for young people prepared to make good use of wider opportunities—never for small children with a day school at hand. I carried a portfolio of attractive Carlisle and Hampton photographs and, while the boys and girls were turning them over, would casually let fall a few words meant to arouse latent interest and ambition.

In three years at White River camp, I had not received so much as a printed circular from the Indian Office, or from the superintendent of Indian schools. I was only once visited by the latter and then in the most perfunctory and mechanical way. I received no instructions whatever, and the most necessary school supplies were issued irregularly, or not at all.

The experience was typical. Each of these little camp schools was an isolated unit, functioning blindly and without standards. The stock excuse of the inefficient teacher was the bald assumption that "Injuns just won't talk American," or "You can't learn them sums; they've not got the head for it." Everything was copied off the board on slates without explanation, and many had no idea of teaching conversational English other than by labored translations from the vernacular.

Incidentally, one may find in a field letter from the Indian Office as recent as November 1935 the statement that "few, if any, of our teachers know how to begin to teach English to a non-English-speaking individual or group." This fundamental problem we pioneers grappled with quite successfully more than half a century ago.

It may be taken for granted that mine was no conventional call some twenty minutes long, ending in a formal handshake and an inscrutable smile. I gave no less than a full day to each little camp school at each visit, and to every boarding school a week or more. Then I offered such encouragement as I honestly could, together with a few constructive suggestions, and repeated their substance in a carefully written letter soon afterward.

In some instances a short program had been memorized for the benefit of a possible caller. The drill ended, the complacent pedagogue would propose adjournment for luncheon and rest. My unexpected reappearance in the schoolroom the minute recess was over no doubt caused him considerable embarrassment. Occasionally, when the work was particularly hopeless, I would offer to teach for a couple of hours. Rather to my surprise the suggestion was usually received with undisguised relief. Probably it excited hopes of witnessing a humiliating failure on the part of this presuming stranger!

One of the most aggravated cases I recall was an attempt to seat about a hundred children, unwashed, uncombed, noisy, and undisciplined, in a schoolroom planned to accommodate fifty. Two were actually assigned to each seat, and when invited to come to the front for a recitation, the youngsters were compelled to scramble over one another's shoulders. The man in charge, originally a trader's clerk, was apparently almost illiterate. Though a good deal disconcerted by my appearance, he bravely called upon a class to rise amid indescribable racket and confusion.

This time I took the drastic step of dismissing one-half the school, had the desks rearranged, placed the one small blackboard in a prominent position, and taught orally for the rest of the morning, utilizing every object and picture I could lay my hands on, introducing marches, motion plays, and action songs, and winning a better response than seemed possible under the circumstances. I advised this man to divide his school into two platoons and to concentrate for the present upon reasonable order and practice in idiomatic English. Too many of the teachers were middle-aged men, not only incompetent but totally unadaptable. Young women as a rule did better. In some cases a couple was employed to good advantage.

Although my office was entirely independent of the local agent (or superintendent), I paid him the courtesy of a prompt call on arrival and another after I had finished my inspection. In a spirit of candor and cooperation I began by giving him a short verbal report of my findings, which, as I shortly discovered, offered the opportunity to counter with a series of diametrically opposed recommendations to Washington. Only one of the five agents with whom I had dealings responded cordially. He was the well-known, successful, and diplomatic Colonel James McLaughlin, afterward an Indian inspector and author of the book *My Friend the Indian*². One man particularly seemed resentful of my unsupervised conversations with the Sioux. He evidently preferred to see all women in properly subordinate positions and was accustomed to have visiting officials dependent upon the use of his own team and the services of his trusted and trained interpreter.

---

1. James McLaughlin (1842–1923), a Canadian by birth, immigrated to the United States in 1863 and was appointed agent at Standing Rock in 1881. *My Friend the Indian*, published in 1910, is an autobiographical and historical account of persons and tribes he was associated with.

A Year on Wheels

On reaching Pine Ridge, the largest Sioux agency, about the middle of June, I decided to call the whole force together July first, when the schools closed for the summer, for an impromptu teachers' institute. There was no time to obtain formal authority from Washington, no precedent for such a move, and, of course, no fund for expenses. I secured the luke-warm consent of the agent and the active aid of the superintendent of the Oglala boarding school, who happened to be a trained man.

We met at his school for three successive days. His best teachers gave demonstrations; the agency doctor and the missionary favored us with talks; and there was open discussion at every point. Here the primitive log day schools were scattered over a radius of seventy-five miles, but every man and woman was in attendance, eager for help. So encouraging was their response, that my report to the Commissioner at the close of the affair brought the hoped-for authorization of a similar gathering at every other agency. Major George Wright of Rosebud hastily nullified the plan by giving all his teachers immediate leave of absence, so that practically all were out of reach by the date named. At the four other agencies meetings were successfully held. They were, I believe, the first of their kind in the Indian Service.

Along this same line, a few were persuaded to subscribe for an educational journal and professional reading circles were organized under the banner of Chautauqua. Two or three accompanied me to the annual meeting of the National Education Association held at Saint Paul in July 1890. All this was utter novelty in the Indian field.

One can hardly wonder that I found the boarding school routine in general drab and lifeless, and the military discipline needlessly harsh. The children had too much drudgery and too little relaxation. They were frequently unhappy and homesick. Some regimentation is no doubt unavoidable in large groups, but one could not but compare these depressing institutions with Hampton, where each individual was loved and studied, with Bishop Hare's homelike, small, church schools, and with the famous "Outing" at Carlisle, giving opportunity for normal home and school life in association with good American farm families.[2]

I was, of course, at once escorted on a formal round and expected to spend so many minutes in each room, to ask a few cut-and-dried questions, listen patiently to the usual requests for transfers, and go quietly away again. My inconvenient habit of dropping in frequently at odd hours, talking privately with pupils, as well as with matron, seamstress, and cook, tasting food prepared for the children, and entering overcrowded dormitories late in the evening to complain of the bad air no doubt seemed to the persons in charge both unnecessary and meddlesome. Bedroom windows, I was informed, must be kept closed and locked, in order to be certain that no boy entered the girls' apartment, and the lack of ventilation was unavoidable, even though, with other unsanitary habits, it helped to spread tuberculosis among healthy children. True, the obvious deficiencies of these institutions were not so much chargeable to the staff, expected to feed, clothe, and teach their charges upon an allowance of some $167.00 per head per annum, as to the negligence and apathy of Congress and the public.

---

2. Under the "outing" system at Carlisle, pupils were placed for the summer, or occasionally longer, with white families near the school. They ordinarily worked as farm or domestic help.

DESERT GARDENS

Now that Captain Pratt's goal of free association and the common school for all Americans
has been in part attained, at least among northern
tribes, let me quote from a private letter of a county
superintendent on what was in my youth the Great
Sioux Reservation. This is what she says of Indian
children in mixed public schools:

> I know that as a race they are capable of anything that
> anyone else is capable of, if they are not trained to think
> otherwise. I can tell as soon as a child walks into one of my
> schools whether he has been attending a boarding school. If
> he has, he is constantly listening for the bell to signal him to
> stand, pass out, eat, wash, rise, pray, and—I am afraid—
> think!

Equally significant is the remark by a woman of
mixed ancestry living in a small town in South
Dakota. Her daughter is in public school and her son
in the state university. "My children," she writes,
"don't know what life is like down among the Indians, and I'll never send them to an Indian school,

as my Dad did. I think the Indian school holds you back so."

It was, of course, as a temporary expedient that we pressed for these schools, with no expectation that they would be needed for more than one generation. Unfortunately, a vested interest has gradually been built up in a policy of segregation and special treatment.

The Jesuits, who controlled, and still control, certain boarding institutions run on the contract plan and therefore subject to official investigation, excelled in nice courtesy and the art of keeping strangers—especially Protestants—at a convenient distance. I found it almost impossible to exceed the conventional routine in visiting these schools. There was, however, abundant evidence of personal devotion and sincere interest in the people. The farms and other industrial features were superior; the girls' needlework beautiful; the academic work, conducted by vested nuns or lay brothers, wooden and old-fashioned. Such was the substance of my criticism which offended ecclesiastics in charge.

Bishop Hare's five schools were maintained by church funds, but until 1901 the children were permitted to draw their treaty rations and annuities at the school, thus reducing the cost of food and clothing. When the contract system was finally abolished, even this small privilege was withdrawn. While the government claimed no jurisdiction in my time, I took pleasure in visiting them regularly and in holding them up as models in most respects. The Bishop's helpers were chosen with clear insight. His active benevolence and good judgment nowhere showed more plainly than in the conduct of these schools. With one exception they were not coeducational, thus eliminating some problems, and the atmosphere, like that of Hampton, was friendly and joyous, rather than arbitrary and mechanical.

Really, the application of progressive ideas to Indian schools is not altogether new. Long ago, I complained that "the gap between natural and formal education is in his case a frightful gulf!" Such influence as I had was steadily exerted in the direction of greater ease, freedom, and vivacity. Meantime, honestly liking the people and the country, I gave myself up to thorough enjoyment along the road.

Few would choose the Sioux reservation as a summer resort—that vast sun-baked region where for days on end no living creature larger than a grasshopper broke the deathlike stillness, and over which I journeyed in a wagon or on ponyback some twenty-four hundred miles in a single season. Yet for me there was an ever fresh charm in selecting a new camping site. It was pleasant to stretch myself on a rug in the shade of the wagon and watch the feeding and grooming of the horses, the pitching of the tipi, the building of a gypsy fire, and the preparation of an al fresco feast. If there were any Sioux in the neighborhood, they were sure to claim kinship with one of us and, on the strength of it, to bring us of their best and be in turn invited to share the rustic meal.

These "gardens of the desert," these "unshorn fields, boundless and beautiful," enjoy the keen thrill of an exhilarating, truly intoxicating climate. Body and spirit are keyed to the pitch of that dry, clear atmosphere and dazzling sunlight. I have walked and ridden in comparative comfort with the mercury at 114 degrees in the shade—and there was no shade. I have also enjoyed a brisk walk in a temperature of 40 degrees below zero—provided there was no wind. One source of exquisite pleasure was the refined, the subtle variety of the prairie landscape. It is an undeveloped taste that complains of monotony in a scene that possesses the grandeur of ocean, with a mellow softness peculiarly its own.

At the time of which I write, there was at Pine Ridge a band of several hundred Northern Cheyennes, who had been captured in desperate flight from Indian Territory and set down on the bare prairie as prisoners of war. With very little help, either from the government or the churches, they had made considerable progress since I first found them huddled together in tipis five years earlier. They were now living in log houses, cultivating small farms, and earnestly pleading for chapels and schools.

Little Wolf, their chief, was a fine-looking man apparently in the prime of life, with a singularly gentle, musical voice and a face full of intelligence and refinement.[1] One day, he called at my temporary log-cabin headquarters near the agency and begged me to visit his people, who, he said, were anxious to meet me.

We did not know the road at all but set out next morning in that general direction, following the usual indefinite prairie trails. Several hours' driving brought us within sight of the White River, here a considerable stream fringed with cottonwoods.The

1. In 1878 a group of Cheyennes under the leadership of Dull Knife and Little Wolf broke away from the Cheyenne and Arapaho agency in Indian Territory and headed north to join their kinsmen at the more northerly agencies. Near Fort Robinson, in northwestern Nebraska, Dull Knife's and Little Wolf's bands separated, the remnants of the former ultimately being interned for a time at Pine Ridge. Little Wolf's band, however, traveled directly to Montana and was never at Pine Ridge. There appears to be a confusion here between Little Wolf and Little Chief, another Cheyenne leader, whose band was permitted a few years later to settle at Pine Ridge (see note 5, p. 28, above).

milky water ran swift and deep. The straggling village lay mainly on the opposite side but our wagon was too heavy and cumbersome to risk the crossing.

We stopped at the nearest house to inquire and found the inmates were Sioux. The son was a returned Carlisle student, who had been severely hurt in an accident, and was glad to meet a friend with whom he could speak English. I promised to send the doctor to see him as soon as I got back and was directed to the home of Little Wolf, near the river bank at the foot of a chalky cliff—a steep descent by no means easy to negotiate. Here we were cordially welcomed by the handsome chief and his family. Mrs. Little Wolf insisted upon putting up our tipi under the trees and brought out a platter of warm fried fish for our supper. Her husband assembled as many men as possible for a council, telling us that the river was unusually high and that not all of them would venture to ford it. A rude bridge had been planned but not yet begun.

A young policeman whose mother was a Dakota and his father a Cheyenne came to interpret. There was true pathos in the sincere plea of these conquered warriors, whose story has been well told by George Bird Grinnell in his book *The Fighting Cheyennes*, for a chance to learn the new way and once more stand as men, among men.[2] Gathered in the one bare room of their leader, seated in kitchen chairs, on iron-hooped trunks, and on the sides of the neatly made beds, they set forth their reasonable plea with the characteristic Indian mingling of simplicity and ceremony. It was something of a novelty for me to hear my words translated from the well-loved Sioux, which I spoke by preference—my driver

2. A natural historian and ethnologist, George Bird Grinnell (1849–1938) based *The Fighting Cheyennes* (1915), still considered a classic account, on many years' acquaintance with the Cheyenne Indians.

spoke good English—into the unfamiliar syllables of the Cheyenne. As Clark Wissler has lately assured us, the Dakota tongue is really an agreeable language, with its many soft consonants, and may live a long time among a few thousand folk who cling to it.[3]

Next morning I was driven for some miles along the top of the bluffs, counting the children and choosing a central and beautiful location for the desired schoolhouse. I was sorry when, within a few months, the order came to transfer the whole band through the blizzards of February to a new home on the Tongue River in Montana.

On our way back to the agency, we stopped by appointment at the school on White Clay Creek to meet in council fifty or more men of that district. They were in a thoroughly dissatisfied frame of mind, seemingly not without good reason. Whatever they may have thought of Washington sending a woman out to confer with them, their attitude was above criticism. I had to explain that I was there to help the schools and had no authority to listen to general complaints or to make general recommendations. Nevertheless, I had no choice but to hear again the old, sorrowful tale of hunger and sickness, unfulfilled promises, untrustworthy servants. Since there was so little I could do about it, the story made me sad at heart.

My next trip took me into a mixed-blood settlement on the edge of the Bad Lands, again to decide upon a suitable location for a new day school. The "squaw men," it appeared, had been unjustly condemned as idle and worthless. I found houses and

---

3. Clark Wissler (1870–1947), an anthropologist long associated with the American Museum of Natural History, was a prolific writer on American Indians.

farms quite equal to those of the average settler. The Sioux women were good housekeepers and neatly dressed, the large families of little ones clean and attractive. All spoke English and seemed ambitious to gain an education.

We spent a day or two exploring the more accessible parts of these strange, fantastically colored cliffs, bare of all verdure, whose towers and spires suggest a ruined city of old time. There were men who made a living by acting as guides to scientific expeditions sent out by the colleges, and by collecting fossils for sale.

There is nothing new about droughts in the Dakotas. By the first of August the tall grass was dry as tinder and prairie fires threatened to destroy the wild hay, upon which local ranchmen depended for winter feed for their stock. We were caught in such a fire and saved barely in time by one of the violent thunderstorms characteristic of that country. In those days, it was sometimes difficult to distinguish a friend from an enemy.

THE BUFFALO ARE COMING!

I HAD COVERED FIVE OF THE SEVEN SIOUX JURIS-
dictions (omitting the Santees of Nebraska) and
reached farthest north at Standing Rock about the
first of October.

The Pratt commission of 1888 had been followed
in the next year by a more successful effort, directed
by General Crook, to purchase nearly half of the vast
wastelands formerly reserved to the Sioux. At about
the same time the huge Territory of Dakota had been
cut in two and two new states admitted to the Union.
However, the rush to homestead claims fell far short
of expectations, aroused to a high pitch by the
tremendous boom in the more fertile and inviting
"Cherokee Strip."[1]

1. In the summer of 1889 the Sioux agreed to sell approximately nine
million acres, largely because of the influence that General George Crook,
who headed the commission, had with the Indians. The sale prices were
somewhat more generous than those offered earlier, and in addition the
government was to provide educational and farming aid and to establish a
three-million-dollar trust fund for the Sioux. The part of the Great Sioux
Reservation retained by the Indians was divided into six separate reservations—Standing Rock, Cheyenne River, Crow Creek, Lower Brulé,
Rosebud, and Pine Ridge. North and South Dakota became states in
November 1889.

The Sioux had naturally hoped for immediate benefit from the reluctant sale of more than nine million acres to which they had clung from sentiment and tradition, although as a matter of fact it was of little use to them without the bison herds that had once covered it. They expected to receive cows, farm tools, and (most pressing at the moment) an increased beef ration. Instead, the issue of beef at the two westernmost agencies was cut from one to two million pounds, causing real privation.[2] The men whose consent to the act had been so lately courted with fair words were ignored and snubbed.

To make matters worse, that summer of 1890 was one of a cycle of dry years, so familiar today. A veritable "Dust Bowl" extended from the Missouri River almost to the Black Hills. In the persistent hot winds the pitiful little gardens of the Indians curled up and died. Even the native hay crop was a failure. I had never before seen so much sickness. The appearance of the people shocked me. Lean and wiry in health, with glowing skins and a look of mettle, many now displayed gaunt forms, lackluster faces, and sad, deep-sunken eyes.

Not until I came to Standing Rock, so far as I remember, did I hear again the fanciful story told one evening by Chasing Crane, twelve months ear-

---

One portion of Indian Territory was opened to settlement in April 1889, and a second, the Cherokee Strip, in 1893. Whatever effect this may have had on settlement in the Dakotas, Elaine Goodale Eastman wrote in the Feburary 1898 issue of *The Advance*: "It now appears that fewer than one million acres [of the former Great Sioux Reservation] have been taken, and that by the poorest of poor people, who are utterly unable to pay the purchase price. . . . The truth of the matter is that the land which appeared so valuable when out of reach is unproductive, semi-arid prairie from which it is well-nigh impossible to wrest a living, at any rate without an expensive system of irrigation. Many claims have already been abandoned" (quoted in Eastman, *Pratt, the Red Man's Moses*, p. 185).

2. Not only were the Sioux disappointed in their expectation of tangible benefits from their land sale, but rations were cut at Pine Ridge and Rosebud after a census showed the population to be smaller than that on which the rations had previously been based.

lier, on the road to the sand hills. We should not lay the Ghost Dance upheaval among the Dakotas solely to the wrongs suffered by them. The touching legend of a Messiah did not originate with them, but crept like a fire in the grass all the way from Mason Valley in Nevada.[3] The story was wonderingly repeated in many tongues beside hundreds of distant campfires, even as far south as Oklahoma. It was more or less seriously accepted in several tribes, but it is true that nowhere except among the wilder bands of Sioux did credulity lead to disaster. The special conditions that existed at Rosebud, Pine Ridge, and Standing Rock— drought, unwise reduction of rations, and dissatisfaction with the results of the last agreement, which many had fought to the end—these made the Dakotas a ready prey to a dangerous illusion. They were the dry grass—tinder dry; the match was the thrilling promise of supernatural help, a Savior for the red man!

With the inevitable tendency to simplify and dramatize history, Commissioner [of Indian Affairs] John Collier and other recent commentators ignore the significant fact that only a small minority, estimated at ten percent, at any time adhered to the "new religion." Even with those few, the movement was in no sense an "outbreak." The eastern groups were unaffected. Educated and Christian Sioux scorned the whole matter. I knew of no church members or returned students who joined the dance. Yet all alike were victims of the natural calamity of the drought and of the broken promises of our government. It might well be said that we wronged the Indians most,

---

3. The Ghost Dance originated with Wovoka (also known as Jack Wilson), a Walker Lake Paiute, who had visions foretelling the peaceful coming of Christ to drive out the white man and bring a return of the bison.

not when we destroyed their wild herds or drove them from their vast ranges, but when we delayed too long the recompense of an equal share in the more advanced culture that inevitably displaced their own.

The early trader Faribault is said to have observed that he counted himself five hundred dollars out of pocket for every Sioux who learned to read and write.[4] And a pioneering missionary has remarked that "if the government had paid the expenses of every Christian mission to Indians, the money would have been well spent, if only as security against war."

It was not the Sioux, as a people, but a small group of the more backward and unenlightened among them, who were carried away some fifty years ago by the promise of a miraculous return to the buffalo days. Nor is it true that, as often asserted, their most celebrated chief, Sitting Bull, was a prophet or leader of the new craze. His biographer, Stanley Vestal, points out correctly that he was among the last of the old leaders to take it up and then with no little hesitation and seeming skepticism.[5] The most that can be shown is that he may have hoped to make use of the movement, already well developed, as a means toward regaining some of his earlier influence.

A party including Short Bull, Kicking Bear, Good Thunder, and one or two more from Rosebud and Pine Ridge had either volunteered or been commissioned to journey over the mountains to look into this strange rumor of a Messiah. They were away for several months and on their return in the spring of 1890 immediately began an active crusade, though

---

4. Probably a reference to either Jean-Baptiste Faribault or his son Alexander (b. 1806), both traders on the Upper Mississippi.

5. See Stanley Vestal, *Sitting Bull, Champion of the Sioux: A Biography* (Boston and New York: Houghton Mifflin, 1932), p. 279.

discouraged by the agent at Pine Ridge to the point of putting one of their number in the guardhouse. Kicking Bear was summoned to Grand River, where Sitting Bull was living, sometime during the summer and about the time of my arrival had begun to instruct the people in the mysteries of the "Spirit Dance." As we learned later, the elaborate rites practiced among the Sioux were a gradual outgrowth of the Messiah idea, invented by its self-constituted high priests in the effort to increase their own importance, and so impress the untutored imagination as to bring about general belief in a promised miracle.

I had found it necessary to change drivers and my new man was a nephew of Sitting Bull. Quite naturally, the chief dined with us in my tent on the golden October day of my visit to Grand River day school. His son Crow Foot (who died with him just over a month later) was a pupil in the school. The old man would not discuss the "new religion" over my beef and bacon, but smilingly professed warm friendship for the white people and in particular a strong inclination toward the church about to hold annual convocation a day's journey from his village.

On the high plateau overlooking Oak Creek, two hundred tents of Christian Indians had been pitched in horseshoe form, almost surrounding the little mission of Saint Elizabeth. Since the chapel could seat only a tithe of the assembled worshipers, most services were held under a rude arbor of freshly cut green boughs. Each evening a ring was formed in the open, in native fashion, for the impressive sunset service, when several white and as many Sioux clergymen in their snowy robes, facing representatives of Bishop Hare's seventeen hundred communicants from all the Dakota agencies, filled the clear air of the high plains with sweetly ordered sounds of praise and prayer.

Meantime, a very different scene was being enacted on the Grand River, forty miles away. It seemed as if a rival religious ceremony had been inaugurated at a dramatic moment and by deliberate design. No Christian chapel, I believe, was ever disturbed by the Ghost Dancers, but they preferred to plant their "sacred tree" as near as possible to church or schoolhouse. They steadily maintained that they, too, worshiped the Christ in this his second appearing!

From Saint Elizabeth's I drove to the nearest day school and found half the children absent with their parents, celebrating the strange rites taught them by Kicking Bear. At the agency everyone was talking of the new craze, treating it as a folly soon to be forgotten. Agent McLaughlin, one of the steadiest and most experienced men in the service, sent his Indian police to forbid the dance and order Kicking Bear to leave the reservation. The prophet left, but the people were in a defiant mood and continued to dance. Merely as a passing novelty, with the added charm of the forbidden, this excitement might easily have served as an outlet for suppressed emotions in a season of gloom and depression.

Unhappily, not all officials could see it in this light. A little later, General Miles took the extraordinary step of authorizing Buffalo Bill, described by the veteran missionary Thomas Riggs as "the doughty hero of the Wild West show," to take Sitting Bull, dead or alive. "This knight of the twentieth century emptied his bottle," wrote Riggs. "A small but select band of fierce cowboys were enlisted, and invited to take a drink. Finally, the very night for the venture was fixed upon—the night for a winter ride of forty miles over the boundless prairie, with glory or death at the break of day!"

Fortunately, the President intervened and called off the comic opera foray barely in time.[6]

My long overland journey to Pine Ridge by the western route over the wildest part of the reservation was uneventful. We camped one night at Big Foot's village, a few miles below the forks of the Cheyenne. Invited to breakfast at the cabin of one of the principal men, we were honorably entertained with pleasant chat over the beef and Indian bread and hot, black coffee. (It would have been the same had these supplies been their last, as they possibly were.) We shook hands cordially with Big Foot, whose real name, however, was Spotted Elk. Little did I dream as we drove gaily out of the peaceful, pretty settlement, its white cones gleaming among yellow cottonwoods, followed by the cheerful barking of many dogs, the laughter of children, and the hearty goodbyes of our kind hosts, that our next meeting—only a few weeks later—would be a tragic one.

A small encampment of the Eighth Cavalry had been for some time stationed just above the forks as a precautionary measure against what some regarded as a threatened "outbreak." I stopped for a word with Colonel [Edwin V.] Sumner and the other officers. They were tired of their lonely post and inclined to

6. Thomas Riggs (1847–1940), son of the pioneer missionary Stephen Return Riggs, worked among the Standing Rock and Cheyenne River Sioux. His Oahe Indian boarding school was located on the Missouri River about sixteen miles northwest of Pierre.

Buffalo Bill Cody, whose Wild West show had once featured Sitting Bull, apparently persuaded General Miles to let him undertake the Indian's arrest. When Cody arrived at Standing Rock with three friends, McLaughlin, who would brook no outside interference, arranged to delay the expedition—first by having officers at nearby Fort Yates entertain the party, and then by making them believe that Sitting Bull had already given himself up at the agency—until he could get the orders canceled. See Utley, *Last Days of the Sioux Nation*, pp. 123–26.

ridicule the notion of danger from the Sioux. Big Foot's people were dancing, certainly; but what of it? Let them enjoy their religion while they could. These army men asserted that they had found Indians more peaceable and more honest than many frontier whites.

Taking the south fork, we forded the shallow windings of the Cheyenne thirty-one times, by actual count, before finally leaving it behind. The Sioux called this performance "threading the needle."

At our last meal on the prairie before reaching Pine Ridge agency, I talked for a long time with Good Thunder, one of the messengers returned from Nevada. He was an old man of winning appearance, with hoary locks that hung nearly to his waist, and the soft voice and ingratiating manner characteristic of many old-time Sioux. I still have my penciled notes of the conversation, made on the spot.

"With three others," said Good Thunder, "I traveled a long time to find the Christ. We crossed Indian reservations and passed through white men's towns. On a broad prairie covered with Indians I saw him at last. We could not tell whence he came. Suddenly he appeared before us—a man of surpassing beauty, with long yellow hair, clad in a blue robe. He did not look at us or speak, but read our thoughts and answered without speech. I saw the prints of the nails on his hands and feet.

"He said that he had come upon the earth once before. Then he had appeared to the white people, who had scorned him and finally killed him. Now he came to red men only. He said their crying had sounded loud in his ears. They were dying of starvation and disease. The Messiah said that he had come to save them. He had thought to come in three days (explaining to me that meant three years) but their cries had so moved him to pity that he would come tomorrow (meaning next summer). He would gather together the souls of all Indians who had died and they would be with the living in Paradise, once more hunting the buffalo, dressing in skins, and dwelling in skin tents as of old. The souls of thieves and murderers must wait for some time outside. The people offered him a pipe, tobacco pouch, and moccasins. He handed the two first to others standing by, but kept the moccasins. Three birds—an eagle, a hawk, and a dove—attended him."

The story is obviously in large part an invention, as we learned later that the original "dreamer" was an illiterate Paiute Indian, known as Wovoka or Jack Wilson—a man subject to trances, possibly a cataleptic. The yellow hair and blue robe, the nail prints and hint of Purgatory are clearly reflected from Christian teachings. The birds and other accessories are typically Indian. All the stories, which were related with a convincing air of sincerity, stressed the return of the buffalo, so necessary to the primitive existence of the plains people. There was no hint of violence or of contemplated war, and no weapons were carried in the dance. Some declared that "a wave of earth" would roll over the cities, leaving the land once more in undisturbed possession of the first inhabitants.

THE GHOST DANCE WAR

THE SIOUX HAD BEEN THOROUGHLY "CON-
quered" in the eighteen-seventies and I had never
considered the possibility of another Indian war. Any
resistance on their part, I knew, must be only a short-
lived revolt led by a handful of hopeless and desperate men. Yet there was a growing sense of fear,
suspicion, and anxiety on all sides. Futile attempts to
forbid the dancing only fanned the flame. Those who
did not dance became gradually infected with a
contagious excitement. The inexperienced agent at
Pine Ridge, a recent political appointee, losing all
control, grew more and more nervous.[1]

None of the missionaries, speaking the language
and knowing the temper of the people as they did,
had the least fear of an uprising. We who loved them
moved among them as freely and with as much

1. Daniel F. Royer became agent at Pine Ridge in October 1890. He was
reportedly called "Young-Man-Afraid-of-Indians" by the resevation's
inhabitants.

confidence as ever. Christian Dakotas constantly pointed out to their wilder kin in friendly and sympathetic fashion the unreality and utter impossibility of the Messiah superstition. "Let the craze run its course and die of itself" was the advice of the more experienced. So said even General [Nelson A.] Miles, in command of the military department of the Missouri, after he had talked with Agent Royer and some of the Indians.

Just at this point an incident occurred which might easily have brought the matter to a head. A young man called Little, who had been for some time evading arrest for some minor offense, was seized by the native police directly in front of the office and in the middle of a dense mass of his friends. It was the day of the "Big Issue," and the place was crowded. Perhaps I have never been in greater danger than at that moment but it was not until some time later that the realization came.

I happened to be crossing the wide plaza alone on my way to the Oglala boarding school, when my attention was caught by a sudden commotion in the crowd. There were angry yells, followed by a sort of harangue delivered in a loud, emphatic voice by a tall Indian standing in the office door. I was too far away to hear the words, but presently the people grew quieter and I passed on, thinking little of it.

Taking advantage of the general state of nerves, this young Little deliberately resisted arrest and called upon his followers for support. "Kill the soldiers (the police)! Kill them all!" was the cry. The representatives of the law were greatly outnumbered; some of the mob were armed; and the agent kept out of sight.

At this juncture a progressive chief named American Horse, appearing unarmed in the doorway, quelled the tumult with a few plain words, telling them that they could easily kill a policeman or two, but that in the end both they and their families would be wiped out by avenging troops. Very possibly he saved all our lives, for if blood had been shed, the action could hardly have been stopped short of a general massacre of whites. However, as a matter of historical fact there was no open violence by the Sioux and no "outbreak" at any time, even after the loss of many Indian lives.

Thomas Riggs, the Congregational missionary who spent his whole life among the Sioux and understood them as well as any man, wrote in *The Advance* the following year: "The dance absorbed all other interests and was so violent to suggest its own remedy. . . . I am ready to say that with proper handling there was nothing to be regarded as specially dangerous, or a serious menace."

Warren K. Moorehead, who visited the center of the disturbance and studied the situation carefully, reported in his book published in 1914, *The American Indian in the United States*:

> The white people became frantic from fear, houses were barricaded and all Indians viewed with suspicion. A sensational press magnified events. . . . No sooner did Indians begin to dance, than Agent Royer bombarded Washington with requests for troops. . . . [The Indians] were in a frenzy. Yet there was no thought of war. [Pp. 107–8, 132]

Mari Sandoz, writing from the settler's point of view in *Old Jules*, testifies thus:

> The first squaw men and breeds that slipped into Rushville and Gordon (Nebraska border towns nearest Pine Ridge) asking protection sent the settlers into a panic. . . . When Agent Royer whipped his lathered team into Rushville, shouting that the Indians were on the warpath, the town loafers fled into the saloons, expecting to hear bloodcurdling whoops at

> their heels. An hour passed, two, and still the plain to the
> north was bare. . . . But Royer had wired for troops and
> would not return to the agency until they came. [Pp. 128–29]

While all this was going on, I set out matter-of-
factly with my Sioux couple and camp outfit on a tour
of inspection among the scattered schools. No courage was required for I had no thought of danger and
regarded the scare-mongers with contempt. I visited
the homes as usual and talked freely with everyone I
met. I was received with the familiar kindness and
treated to pounded meat with cherries and other
native delicacies.

There was no secrecy about the dance which had
caused such frantic alarm. It was held in the open,
with neither fire nor light, after the participants had
fasted for a day or two and passed through the
purifying ordeal of the sweat-lodge. Anyone might
look on, and on a bright November night I joined a
crowd of spectators near Porcupine Tail Butte—the
only person who was not a Sioux.

Under the soft glow of the hunter's moon perhaps
a hundred men, women, and children, with clasped
hands and fingers interlocked, swung in a great circle
about their "sacred tree," chanting together the monotonous Ghost Dance songs. The hypnotic repeti-
tion of the words: "Once more we shall hunt the
buffalo—Our Father has said it!" alternated with
short invocations by prophet or priest and occasional
intervals of wailing by the women—that musical
heart-piercing sound which, once heard, is never
forgotten. No one with imagination could fail to see
in the rite a genuine religious ceremony, a faith
which, illusory as it was, deserved to be treated with
respect.

"You have your churches; why can we not have
ours?" was the natural reaction of the people.

In the course of an hour or two, one of the worshipers would break abruptly from the ring, rush wildly about, and fall in a trance or faint, lying for some time motionless. One old woman fell so near me that I could have touched her. Presently she stirred, got to her feet unaided, and addressed the gathering in a strong voice:

"My children, I have seen those dear ones we lost long ago!"

"Ah-h-h! He-ye-ye!" responded the people.

"They are living in a most beautiful country covered with buffalo!"

"He-ye-ye! Ate heye lo!" (Our Father has said it.)

"Their tipis are of skins. They are feasting and playing. They are perfectly happy!" (After each statement the people intone their deep-voiced response.)

"Here everything looks hateful to me—how can I bear it!"

The congregation responds with groans and cries. Then the priest repeats that the Messiah will appear "with the new grass" in spring and the vision will come true for all believers.

After listening to this strange litany for half the night, I lay down in my tent quite worn out with sympathetic excitement. The spell, or incantation, or rite continued with increasing fervor until dawn.

The prophets of the Messiah now began to instruct their converts that they should throw away everything brought by the white man, wear only native dress, and revive the old, obsolete customs. While there was a noticeable trend in this direction, it was impossible to conform strictly. Knives, kettles, cotton cloth, blankets, and flour—to mention only a few items—had long since become indispensable. Some bows and arrows were made. One woman, recovering from her trance, announced that she had been told of a garment that all must wear. It was a shirt for men, a robe for women, fashioned of coarse unbleached muslin, heavily fringed and painted in symbolic figures. It was supposed to be sewed with sinew for thread. This tawdry imitation of the departed skin clothing was typical of the whole pitiful delusion. After troops had come it was asserted that the "sacred shirts" were bullet-proof.

Moving on to the Medicine Root, some fifty miles from the agency, I received a call from the wife of Little Wound, the local chief. Excitedly she defended the new cult, in which her husband had become a leader and which was opposed by a strong party of native Christians headed by the Reverend Amos Ross.

On this same evening Little Wound himself approached the day school teacher and indignantly demanded of him why soldiers were coming. The troops so insistently demanded by the agent had in fact reached Rushville (at least seventy miles from Medicine Root) that very evening. An all-night march brought them to the agency by daybreak the next morning. But neither of us had heard of this nor could we guess how Little Wound knew.

All employees in the outlying districts now received peremptory orders to report immediately at the agency. The teacher taught half a day for my benefit before setting out on horseback. That night there was dancing again and I slept quietly in my tent within a few rods of hundreds of excited worshipers. Thrilling cries and the dull beat of many moccasined feet mingled strangely with my dreams.

While we sat at breakfast in the open, a native policeman who had ridden all night brought me a polite note from the agent, requesting an immediate interview. I never learned why I had not been recalled at the same time as the others. Possibly Mr. Royer supposed that I would take fright and come in without being sent for. Perhaps he did not feel responsible for the safety of an independent government officer. Or he may have resented the casual way in which I mingled with the people.

I soon found that this time the whole population had been ordered in. There was great commotion—ponies hurriedly caught, tents razed, goods packed, and the roads were soon black with long convoys moving in two different directions. There was nothing for me to do in a deserted camp. Reluctantly I gave the order and we covered the fifty miles before sunset.

Now that troops were actually quartered at the agency the unexpected order to "come in" had divided the Sioux. Many families were broken up and feeling was intense. Submission was easy for the "church party," but the Ghost Dancers who had defied police authority, fearing summary punishment, fled in terror to the Bad Lands. From that seventeenth day of November on, the thousands encamped close about the agency were known as the "friendlies." Those poor creatures who retreated in desperation to their natural fortress, subsisting miserably on such part of the government herd as they had been able to carry away, were dubbed "hostiles"—although they had committed no hostile act. The truth is that their flight was merely a stampede and there were no raids whatever outside the reservation.

It was a time of grim suspense. We seemed to be waiting—helplessly waiting—as if in some horrid nightmare, for the inevitable catastrophe. It seems to me today that I have already lived once through the European situation, where nations armed to the teeth confront one another in mutual dread and mutual menace. Something like it, on a far smaller scale, was that tragic Christmas season of 1890 among the Sioux. Then, as now, it seems that two or three men in positions of power could swiftly break the evil spell. No one wanted war—unless it were a few border towns, who saw a cash market for local produce and a chance of taking over in the end the lands they coveted. All Indian wars had ended so.

We were practically under martial law. The infantry, in their neat Sibley tents, encamped in our midst, surrounded themselves with trenches and impromptu breastworks. A buffalo-coated sentinel, rifle on shoulder, met us at every turn. We gathered daily in little groups to watch the troops parade, but there was some unvoiced resentment, especially when the order was given to admit no Sioux within picket lines after half past four, putting a stop to Mr. Cook's nightly vesper service.

I had been urged to make my headquarters at the rectory and was living there with my dear friends, Mr. and Mrs. Cook, and their little boy throughout these troubled weeks. Himself half Sioux, the minister was visibly torn between his natural sympathies and his loyalty to the government. He was constantly busy—talking with police, army officers, press correspondents, going about the camps with food, medicines, practical help, and religious consolation. Day by day his fine features sharpened; his eyes, burning and black, sank deeper in his head; and no self-control could keep the strain entirely out of his voice.

Dr. Eastman, a Sioux of an Eastern band, fresh from medical school in Boston and unacquainted with reservation life, had taken on the duties of agency physician at this precise juncture. I had read of his college career in a chance newspaper clipping, had several times met his brother, the Reverend John Eastman, and had looked forward with more than common interest to our meeting. After that first evening, an invitation affair, he came often to the rectory, and I helped carry food and other little comforts to his patients in their cotton tents, where the sick and little ones suffered keenly from exposure. The grazing near at hand was soon exhausted; ponies were half starved; the people were restless and unhappy. Standing, as they did, between the whites and the Ghost Dance party, police, mixed-bloods, and members of the church were often threatened with reprisals from the latter and were probably in greater danger than any of us.

Week after week the unnatural tension persisted. Swarms of "war correspondents" from New York, Chicago, and western cities could hardly be blamed for inventing sensational stories in default of news. Yet their highly colored dispatches increased alarm and deepened prejudice against the Sioux. Army officers frankly admitted that "the army doesn't know what it is here for" and even asserted that "these Indians don't deserve punishment," but we heard that the men were bored with inaction and spoiling for a fight.

Like the missionaries I resented the soldiers and was deeply sympathetic with the Sioux. My driver had near kin among the refugees in the Bad Lands, whom he visited secretly at night, bringing me private bulletins. He asserted that if arrests were attempted the young men would resist. The whole situation was intolerable.

Father Jutz, the good German priest in charge of the Catholic mission school five miles out, declined military protection and not only kept a hundred children safe throughout the disturbance, but fed and sheltered many fugitives.[2] He went fearlessly among the so-called "hostiles" in the effort to bring about a peaceful surrender, and this not without effect. Small parties came in from time to time to "council" with General [John R.] Brooke, the officer in charge. Others roamed the outlying districts and, compelled by hunger, now and then raided the homes and the herds of the "friendly" group, encamped much against their will in our immediate neighborhood. I pleaded in vain that they be allowed to go home, that normal conditions be restored as far as possible and the day schools reopened.

2. Father John Jutz, some seventy years of age and a German Tyrolean by birth, was in charge of the Holy Rosary (or Drexel) Mission.

WOUNDED KNEE

WHAT HAPPENED NEXT WAS HARDLY THE FAULT of the army over and above other branches of the government, yet for many years I had only painful associations with the sight of my country's trig dark-blue uniform. It had for me no glamor whatever, and the tentative addresses of one young officer whom I met first at Standing Rock and again at Pine Ridge were discouraged with unnecessary abruptness.

We who really knew and loved the Sioux were convinced that, with patience and redress of their grievances, the sane and loyal majority might safely be counted upon to bring a fanatical few to their senses. It cannot be too clearly understood that the clash was between two cultures—not two races. The cause of the pretended Messiah was already lost and time was on our side.

Autumn glided imperceptibly into winter and still the prairies were brown and bare. The hazy mildness of a late Indian summer lingered on into the Advent season—a brief triumph for the followers of the new religion. Their priests had asserted that so long as the people continued to dance there would be no snow, and the return of the buffalo was definitely promised with the new grass in spring. When these promises were seen to fail (we reasoned), then surely faith in miracles would die and the crowds of hysterical dancers would melt away.

Strong in this hope, we went on with our accustomed plans for the Christmas season of peace and good-will. The trader's family and the wives of some of the employees were leaving hurriedly on various excuses, but the teachers stuck bravely to their posts. The doors of the large Oglala boarding school were kept locked by day as well as by night and the grounds, surrounded by a high fence of barbed wire, constantly patrolled by armed guards. These boys and girls, held partly as hostages for the good behavior of their parents, in part for their own protection, must be fed, taught, and kept in order.

The needs of the loyal and Christian element in their crowded, insanitary camps were pressing upon us, while at the moment we were unable to do anything for those stubborn ones who persistently refused to "come in." General Brooke strictly forbade all unauthorized communication with the Bad Lands.

Accordingly, native cedar was woven into spicy garlands for the adornment of the chapel. Boxes of clothing and toys were opened and sorted for distribution, money was collected among our visitors for the purchase of oranges and candy, and Christmas carols practiced nightly. In the midst of the pleasant, familiar stir, centering in the little brown church on the hill and the snug rectory close by, came the breathtaking news of the death of Sitting Bull, while resisting arrest at his home on the Grand River, two hundred miles away.

The seizure and confinement of the supposed leaders in any mischief that might be on foot was the traditional military method of heading off further trouble. In this instance as in others, it led promptly to the very crisis it intended to avert! McLaughlin, agent at Standing Rock, in his way an able executive, hated and distrusted Sitting Bull, whom he had long tried to suppress. While stigmatizing him as a coward and a faker, McLaughlin's real fear of the chief was plainly shown at this juncture. He repeatedly urged that the old man with a few other potential "trouble makers" be removed from the reservation and shut up where they could do no harm. The proposed imprisonment—fearful punishment for an Indian, dreaded more than death—was to be based solely on suspicion.

The dictator of Standing Rock, who had resented the noisy and presumptuous entrance of Buffalo Bill upon the scene, did not, like Royer, invite military interference. He insisted throughout that he could handle the situation without help and that his well-trained police might be trusted to carry out his orders. He probably believed that they would take the chief into custody without causing grave disturbance. After considerable delay and hesitation on the part of the authorities, he was permitted to make the attempt. It led, unhappily enough, to the tragedy of a patriot's death at the hands of his own people, with the sacrifice of the lives of six brave native police in the line of duty, and—as a fairly direct consequence—to the many times multiplied tragedy of Wounded Knee.

Regular troops sent from Fort Yates to support the police not only failed to arrive in time to be of any use, but actually mistook the surviving bluecoats around Sitting Bull's cabin for hostiles and hurled shells on them from a distance, fortunately doing no damage.[1]

While the killed and wounded on the government side were conveyed to the agency in wagons, together with the mutilated body of the chief, the Grand River people left their own dead on the field (to be buried later by the courageous missionary Thomas Riggs), and in desperate panic stampeded southward. Some of them presently went back; others took refuge with their kinsfolk under Big Foot, near the forks of the Cheyenne. When Colonel Sumner chided the chief for taking them in, he replied simply that they were his brothers who had come to him hungry, footsore, and almost naked, that he had received and fed them, and that no one with a heart could have done less.

It seems, however, that the panic of the poor fugitives proved contagious, for after one day's travel in the direction of their own agency (the Cheyenne River), they halted to talk matters over and were surrounded by Sumner's command, the same officer I had seen and talked with a few weeks earlier. They were marched back up the Cheyenne, apparently in the direction of Fort Meade. The same missionary before mentioned has asserted in print that "their capture was an outrage and their escape a disgrace!" They had committed no fault and were obeying orders when arrested and turned about, presumably that they might be confined at the fort. In the end

---

1. McLaughlin ordered a contingent of about fifty Indian police to arrest Sitting Bull at his home on the Grand River early in the morning of December 15. Although the chief at first appeared to be willing to go along peacefully, a scuffle broke out and Sitting Bull and his son Crow Foot were killed. In the ensuing exchange of shots, six of Sitting Bull's followers in the crowd that had gathered, as well as six Indian police, were killed.

they were left without a guard at their own village with orders to report early next day to the commanding officer and surrender their guns.

"This meant gross carelessness and extreme verdancy," Riggs declares. By this time they had, of course, become thoroughly frightened, and thought only of escape. Some beef cattle were killed for food and the whole party was under way that same evening, moving blindly toward the main body of refugees in the Bad Lands.

Sitting Bull fell dead among his family and supporters early in the morning of December fifteenth. Excited and more or less garbled stories of the event, with its train of alarming consequences, naturally deepened our anxiety at Pine Ridge. Far from lessening the tension, it seemed to make further disaster almost inevitable.

We were not taken into the confidence of General Brooke and did not know that a detachment of the Seventh Cavalry—Custer's old command—had been sent under Major [Samuel M.] Whitside to meet and disarm the approaching band of fugitives. After he had taken them into camp on Wounded Knee Creek there came a request for reinforcements. Colonel [James W.] Forsyth joined Whitside with four additional troops and four pieces of light artillery, making a total of 470 well-armed men, well fed and warmly clothed, to oppose an unorganized mob of something over three hundred ragged, hungry, and frightened men, women, and children.

At this point there were actually no Indians left in the Bad Lands. Kicking Bear, Short Bull, and their followers had gradually yielded to persuasion and were encamped near the Catholic mission, only five miles from the agency. This meant that if a violent clash could be avoided reconciliation was at hand.

A large Christmas tree had been set up in the church and it was planned to dress and illuminate it on several successive evenings for several separate congregations represented in the "friendly" camp. We were marking gifts and filling candy bags on the morning of the twenty-ninth of December, when the distant thunder of big guns, some eighteen miles away, sent cold shivers down our backs. Within an incredibly short time came first reports of the slaughter at Wounded Knee. We were told, indeed, that the cavalry had been cut off from reaching us and that we were at the mercy of a maddened horde of Indians!

When the loyal Sioux heard that unarmed men, women, and children had been shot down without pity, they were wild with fear. Their white camps melted away like snow in the sun. The brown hills were instantly alive with galloping horsemen, the loaded wagons following them. The troops had been so widely scattered at strategic points that only a small guard of infantry remained to protect the agency. Toward evening some outlying buildings were fired and there was an exchange of shots. Everything indicated the probability of a night attack in force with small chance of escape.

The mission house and church was packed with crying and terrified women and children, for the most part of mixed blood. Real though I knew the danger to be, while shutters were slammed and thin lines of soldiers thrown out on all sides, it was impossible to forget that the "rebels," too, were our friends. I doubt if a single teacher or missionary sought to arm himself in this hour, or could have fired at a Sioux to save his own life. Mrs. Cook and I, inwardly strung up, moved among the fugitives with hot coffee and sandwiches and comforting words.

Of course, no one thought of sleep. That night and for several more nights we lay down in our clothes, half expecting to be aroused before dawn. Long after dark the Seventh Cavalry appeared, bringing their own dead and wounded and thirty-three Dakotas, most of them severely wounded women and children. I can never forget Mr. Cook's incredulous horror when he came upon the poor creatures in their bloody rags, huddled on the bare boards of several army wagons, chilled to the bone and too stunned in their culminating misfortunes to utter a sound, until the torture of fresh movement wrung from them screams of agony.

The horses had been taken out and the helpless prisoners left alone in the darkness and cold, while army surgeons were busy with their own wounded, about thirty in number. For these all available tents were urgently required and the few civilians left at Pine Ridge were for the most part fully occupied with concern for their own safety.

The Dakota clergyman acted with humanity. Those refugees who had sought sanctuary in the church were sent to a nearby log house. Pews were torn from their fastenings and armfuls of hay fetched by Indian helpers. Upon a layer of this we spread quilts and blankets taken from our own beds. The victims were lifted as gently as possible and laid in two long rows on the floor—a pitiful array of young girls and women with babes in arms, little children, and a few men, all pierced with bullets or terribly torn with pieces of shell, and all sick with fear.

Mr. Cook sought the doctor of their own blood and asked General Brooke to place him formally in charge of the emergency hospital, which was done at once. With such volunteer help as was at hand, Dr.

Eastman worked through the night. When an army doctor appeared with the dawn to assist, the Sioux women were, quite understandably, so terrified of the uniform that he had great difficulty in approaching them.

"Yes, yes, take it off! It is worthless!" screamed one poor girl whose "sacred robe," now torn and spotted with her blood, had wholly failed to protect her from the storm of flying steel. But the invincible modesty of the women who, even in extreme straits clung frantically to their rags, proved no slight obstacle to the work of relief. We made gallons of hot coffee and from some source—perhaps the boarding school—managed to requisition enough bread to feed them all. By the next day we had obtained fresh beef, and set up a soup kitchen and a bakery in the rectory.

If the long period of suspense had passed like a dream, these next few days were nothing short of nightmare. Our patients cried and moaned incessantly, and every night some dead were carried out. In spite of all we could do, most of the injuries proved fatal. The few survivors were heartbroken and apathetic, for nearly all their men had been killed on the spot. The tree was dragged out, but joyous green garlands still wreathed windows and doors, while the glowing cross in the stained glass window behind the altar looked down in irony—or in compassion—upon pagan children struck down in panic flight.

AN END AND A BEGINNING

THE WOUNDED KNEE AFFAIR WAS REPRESENTED by Colonel Forsyth, officer in charge, as a "gallant" action by brave men, in which "comparatively few squaws" were injured. When Commissioner Morgan asked for my version, I sent him a letter based upon my personal interviews with survivors, the reports of eye-witnesses, and Dr. Eastman's account of his visit to the field on January first to look for any wounded who might still be alive. The Commissioner gave it to the New York papers, where it appeared under the heading:

MISS GOODALE BLAMES THE TROOPS FOR THE KILLING
OF WOMEN AND CHILDREN

The testimony of the survivors of Big Foot's band (the letter ran in part) is unanimous on one important point—namely, that the Indians did not deliberately plan a resistance. The party was not a war party, according to their statement—which I believe to be true—but a party intending to visit the agency upon the invitation of Red Cloud. The Indians say that many of the men were unarmed. When they met the troops, they anticipated no trouble. The demand for their arms was a surprise, but the majority chose to submit quietly. The tipis had already been searched and a number of knives, guns and hatchets confiscated, when the searching of the persons of the men was begun. The women say that they, too, were searched, and the knives which they always carry for domestic purposes taken from them. A number of the men had surrendered their rifles and cartridge belts when one young man, described by the Indians as a good-for-nothing young fellow, fired a single shot. This called forth a volley from the troops and the firing and confusion became general.

I do not credit the statement which has been made by some, that the women carried arms and participated actively in the fight. There may have been one or two isolated cases of this kind, but there is no doubt that the great majority of the women and children, as well as many unarmed men and youths had no thought of anything but flight. They were pursued up the ravines and shot down indiscriminately by the soldiers. The killing of women and children was in part unavoidable, owing to the confusion, but I think there is no doubt that it was in many cases deliberate and intentional. . . .

The party of scouts who buried the dead report eighty-four bodies of men and boys, forty-four of women, and eighteen of young children. Some were carried off by the hostiles. A number of prisoners, chiefly women, have since died of their wounds and more will soon follow. The party who visited the battle field on January first to rescue any wounded who might have been abandoned, and who brought in seven, report that nearly all the bodies of the men were lying close about Big Foot's tent, while the women and children were scattered along a distance of two miles from the scene of the encounter. . . . The irresponsible action of one hot-headed youth should not be the signal for a general and indiscriminate slaughter of the unarmed and the helpless.

I think the Sioux story of Wounded Knee is now generally accepted, but at the time it was strongly resented by military authorities and every effort was made to suppress or discredit it. I was myself censured for putting it into circulation. When the facts could no longer be successfully denied, the absurd explanation was put forward that the "squaws" looked so much like warriors that the soldiers could not tell them apart! An equally ridiculous excuse was the implication that, because some of the women had their skinning knives, they were therefore active combatants.

It must be borne in mind that the Hotchkiss guns were trained directly on the tipis in which the Sioux had spent the night. In one lay the chief, Big Foot, seriously ill with what appears to have been pneumonia. The rag of white cloth, which they had raised as soon as they caught sight of Forsyth's command, still flew above it when the tent was set on fire by the shells and burned above the sick man's head.

The males of all ages from fifteen to seventy, a few more than a hundred in number, had been lined up and completely encircled by soldiers. Mr. Riggs, who knew them well, thought that not more than half were armed. Therefore, after they had delivered up forty or more old guns (General Miles reported forty-eight surrendered), it is certain that very few remained in their hands. It is the inevitable conclusion that the sixty or more casualties among the troops were for the most part victims of their comrades' rifles. Their disposition was such that this misfortune could hardly have been avoided. This point has generally been ignored by historians. Forsyth was tried by court-martial for his conduct of the Wounded Knee affair but was exonerated.

On the third day after the fight (more justly termed a massacre), while small parties of disaffected Indians were still roving about and making sporadic attacks, Dr. Eastman obtained permission to go in search of possible survivors who might not have been able to get away. He took with him about a hundred civilians, most of them Sioux. The position of the bodies proved beyond question that women carrying babies, or with small children clinging to their skirts, were chased and struck down a mile or two from the site of the camp. On that desolate field the frozen bodies lay thick, or piled one on another, under a blanket of fresh snow, among fragments of burned tents and other goods.

"It took all my nerve," wrote the Doctor in his life story, *From the Deep Woods to Civilization,* "to keep my composure in the face of this spectacle, and of the excitement and grief of my companions, nearly every one of whom was crying aloud or singing his death song."

Mooney errs in stating that the burial party of soldiers and scouts brought in some wounded.[1] This was done earlier by the civilian group of volunteers, who found seven still alive. Most of them succumbed later, but one baby, taken from her dead mother's arms, was adopted and educated by General [L. W.] Colby of the Nebraska state troops. The "Lost Bird," as she was called, died a few years ago, after marriage to a Californian.

Some ghastly photographs were taken of corpses in grotesque and tortured attitudes, piled on wagons like so much cordwood, from which they were thrown into a common pit. It was reliably reported that certain white men stripped bodies before burial and carried away "ghost shirts" and other articles as mementoes. Lack of decency in the disposal of the dead is commented upon with some bitterness by Mooney, who criticizes the missionaries at the agency for failing to be present, to read the prayers of the

---

1. Anthropologist James Mooney investigated the Ghost Dance and the Wounded Knee tragedy under the auspices of the Bureau of American Ethnology. His report, "The Ghost-Dance Religion and the Sioux Outbreak of 1890," was published in the *Fourteenth Annual Report of the Bureau of American Ethnology* (Washington, D.C., 1896).

church. Yet would not a religious service under the circumstances have been something of a mockery?

Absorbed in caring for the innocent victims, we were saved from dwelling upon further danger to ourselves. Two Presbyterian missionary women and "Bright Eyes" (then Mrs. Tibbles), a visitor from the Omahas, promptly offered their services at the emergency hospital.[2] Considerable bodies of troops were rushed to the scene, and I vividly recall the coming of the Ninth Cavalry as it galloped past the church early in the morning after the fight, the Negro soldiers uttering savage yells. Far from regarding them with gratitude as our protectors, it must be admitted that our sentiments were mixed with indignation.

Appeals published in the Boston papers brought generous supplies of clothing, blankets, and linen for dressings. Clean cots soon replaced matted heaps of hay and a trained nurse was finally installed. Meantime, two or three thousand Sioux who had been on the point of surrender before Wounded Knee fell back on the White Clay and proposed to die fighting. It was no easy matter to convince them that it was not the intention of the government to disarm and then massacre them all.

Stunning as was the impact upon our nerves of the spectacle of extreme agony and violent death, there was still deeper tragedy in the psychological reactions of Dakotas who had freely accepted our religion and culture. Many of them had white fathers, and in practically every case they remained loyal to govern-

2. Bright Eyes (Susette La Flesche Tibbles) was an educated Omaha Indian well known in humanitarian circles. She had played a central role in seeking redress for the Poncas, forcibly removed from their lands to a reservation in Indian Territory in the late 1870s, and later married Omaha newspaperman Thomas Henry Tibbles, who was also involved in the case.

ment and church. Theirs, however, was a bitter mental struggle which Mr. Cook, for one, survived less than two years. The native police were objects of passionate abuse and threats from their wilder kin, and all of the "friendlies" suffered a great deal of unnecessary hardship and loss.

The strain of waiting for possible further clashes was severe. Early in January 1891, General Miles assumed personal command at Pine Ridge, where he entered upon a campaign of patient conciliation. Rations were increased about one-third and practically everything promised that the Sioux had asked. (We wondered why this could not have been tried before calling upon the War Department.)

Good Father Jutz was among the emissaries bearing offers of amnesty and overtures of peace to the hostile camp. More than two weeks after Wounded Knee these offers were finally accepted. A forlorn and weary cavalcade, said to number over two thousand men, women, and children, trailed in over the snowy ridges—a sight long to be remembered. About twenty leaders were confined for a few months in Fort Sheridan [Illinois] and then released.

The cost of this affair in lives was about three hundred Sioux, and forty-nine soldiers and others on the government side. In money, Mooney estimates it at one million, two hundred thousand dollars.

The unprovoked murder of a Sioux called Few Tails on January eleventh, when he was returning from a hunt in the Black Hills on a pass from his agent, knowing nothing of any trouble, forms a suggestive footnote. Not only was this harmless old man shot down by two white men, but his wife was wounded and a companion, One Feather, with wife and two children, chased and repeatedly fired at by the same heartless wretches, who were never even tried for the crime!

The gift of myself to a Sioux just at this crisis in their affairs will seem to some readers unnatural. Others will find it entirely human and understandable. In reality, it followed almost inevitably upon my passionate preoccupation with the welfare of those whom I already looked upon as my adopted people.

Though I had not consciously considered marriage with a Dakota, I had closely observed several such marriages which appeared successful. The idea certainly did not repel me in any way.

Dr. Eastman, as I have said, was appointed government physician at Pine Ridge at about the time of my return from a round of inspection at the other Sioux agencies. He was warmly welcomed by my friends, Mr. and Mrs. Cook. It seemed that we were from the first mutually attracted. Others have found me cold, distant in manner, and unduly grave, but to him, as he once said, it seemed as if I carried on my heart the sorrows of his people.

Events threw us together. His energy and zeal were in striking contrast with the apathy of the average agency doctor of that day. He completely reorganized his office, requisitioned more adequate medical supplies, and bought a saddle horse with his own money in order that he could respond to distant calls. Up to that time no transportation was furnished, there was neither hospital nor nurse, and medical care was really a farce on the larger agencies.

When I accidently learned that the Doctor had been up all night with a sick baby, I was deeply touched by this quite ordinary incident. Together, we drove out to inspect the Catholic mission, and the good Father had his two guests served with a solitary luncheon, in the course of which we became much better acquainted. He told me his age, then nearly thirty-three, and something of his history.

His mother's father, Captain Seth Eastman (later distinguished as a painter of Indian life), had been an army officer at Fort Snelling, Minnesota, where he fell in love with the pretty daughter of Chief Cloudman and a daughter, Nancy, was born. She, at the age of about sixteen, had eloped with one of the leading warriors, but died a dozen years later following the birth of her youngest son, Ohiyesa. Separated from his father in the turmoil and desperation of the Minnesota massacre, this four-year-old boy had been carried off by an uncle into the wilds of Manitoba. There he never saw a schoolhouse or heard English spoken until sought and found by his father, Many Lightnings. Converted in the meantime to Christianity and a farmer, he had taken his wife's surname and was called Jacob Eastman. Ohiyesa was then fifteen years of age.

Since that time he had been almost continuously in school and college with young people of the dominant race. His own kin were independent citizen Sioux and had never been time-serving "agency Indians."[3]

We became engaged under the Christmas tree he had helped me trim for the children of "our people," who, shivering in their cotton tipis, still awaited we

3. Charles Eastman (Ohiyesa) later recorded the story of his life in *Indian Boyhood* (1902) and *From the Deep Woods to Civilization* (1916). His father, Jacob Eastman (Many Lightnings), had been among the Santee Sioux imprisoned at Davenport, Iowa, after the Sioux Uprising of 1862. On his release from prison, where he had converted to Christianity, the elder Eastman had joined a group of Santees who chose to break their tribal ties by taking homesteads near Flandreau on the Big Sioux River, some forty miles north of Sioux Falls.

knew not what disaster. After seven years' travel "in a strange country," another untried road stretched out before this adopted member of the Lame Horse band.

EPILOGUE

WHEN, ONLY A FEW WEEKS AFTER OUR FIRST meeting, I promised to marry Dr. Eastman, it was with a thrilling sense of two-fold consecration. I gave myself wholly in that hour to the traditional duties of wife and mother, abruptly relinquishing all thought of an independent career for the making of a home. At the same time, I embraced with a new and deeper zeal the conception of life-long service to my husband's people. How simple it all seemed to me then—how far from simple has been the event!

From blazing a new path I returned to the old and well-worn road, trodden by women's feet throughout the ages. That first little home built for us, the center of so many loving hopes, was sorrowfully abandoned within two years for what proved to be a series of dubious experiments. Unforeseen complications led to repeated changes of occupation and of scene, trying to the spirit no less than to the pocketbook. Of my six children, two were born in the Indian country, nine years apart, two in St. Paul, Minnesota, two in New England.

The Doctor practiced medicine in a city as well as among his own people—but not for long. Three years he traveled in the United States and Canada for the International YMCA. For two winters we lived in Washington, where he lobbied for Indian claims. After several other abortive efforts, we finally made a home in Massachusetts where we could educate our family. In an hour of comparative leisure I had urged him to write down his recollections of the wild life, which I carefully edited and placed with *St. Nicholas*. From this small beginning grew *Indian Boyhood* and eight other books of Indian lore, upon all of which I collaborated more or less. Their wide acceptance led to a demand for lectures by the author, and for fifteen years I handled nearly all the correspondence and publicity incident to twenty-five or more annual appearances.

No, I won't say that the adjustment was easy or that I was never lonely, restless, and haunted by a secret sense of frustration. Every woman who has surrendered a congenial task and financial independence will understand. Saving the joys of motherhood, my pleasures must be vicarious ones. He traveled widely, even to London, and met hosts of interesting people. I was inevitably house-bound. But I had always something of a one-track mind, and for many a year every early dream and ambition was wholly subordinated to the business of helping my talented husband express himself and interpret his people. Whether or not this was wise is perhaps an open question. Obviously, it was far from modern. Moreover, it had never been my mother's attitude, but was doubtless in my blood, as a leading tenet of both grandmothers. I was conscious, half proudly, half with regret, of deserting literature for life. Yet my own son calls that "impossible!"

"You've always been a poet," he writes, "whether you put the words on paper or not." (A charming bit of flattery, which I should much like to deserve!)

I did, in fact, produce a few "pot-boilers," for our income was never at all adequate to the family needs, in spite of my husband's varied activities and growing reputation. In odd hours I wrote several fanciful plays and pageants, and published four books for young folks: *Little Brother o' Dreams* (1910), *Yellow Star* (1911), *Indian Legends Retold* (1919), and *The Luck of Oldacres* (1928), embodying some of the lighter and more joyous phases of a strenuous experience.[1]

There were, of course, my exacting duties as nurse and housekeeper to a family of eight. In addition, I prepared four of my children to enter school at varying points between the second and fifth grades— this at periods when no suitable school was available. As they grew up, the financial strain grew more severe with the need of carrying forward their education beyond the high school. For ten years I carried the more burdensome responsibilities of a summer camp for girls in New Hampshire—a job undertaken when past fifty with the help of my older girls and for their benefit, but which also proved of value to me in many ways, bringing new contacts and developing unsuspected capacities.

Social service and civic undertakings have always been most congenial, but only "by fits and starts" has it been possible for me to cooperate locally. Of pure recreation there has been so little in my life that I have never really learned to play. I count myself

---

1. *The Voice at Eve* was published in 1930 and *Hundred Maples* and *Pratt, the Red Man's Moses* in 1935.

fortunate in my children—doubly blessed in my grandchildren—and not least in the memory of a gifted daughter whose golden voice and personality had already won marked recognition at twenty-four, when she fell a victim to the pandemic of influenza following the war. . . . Nor am I ready to admit, with certain of my thoroughly disillusioned contemporaries, that God has left his heaven and all's wrong with the world.